# Break that Curse!
# Get Rid of the Evil Spirits,
# Demons, and Ghosts.

## *The How-To Book*
## *on Deliverance*

By: Ramsey Crowell

# Acknowledgments

First of all, I want to thank my prayer team for their covering me with prayer as I wrote this book. They are my oldest son, Joshua, my oldest daughter, Lycia, my youngest son, Kyle, and a dear saint at the church my brother pastors named Lenny.

Next I want to give a special thanks to my daughter Lycia for taking the time to proofread and correct my grammatical mistakes. When I sent her my first draft, it came back with red all over it. I corrected it and sent it back and she changed some more things on it. She has an 18-month old child and I know it was hard for her to set in front of the computer that long. However, she did it for her dear old dad, and I am most appreciative of it. Without her and my prayer team, this would have been a flop.

I also want to thank my family physician, Khavar J. Dar M.D. He has not only been a great physician watching over me physically, but a caring friend as well. My thanks also go out to Mary Beth Cishek, M.D.

I also want to thank my beautiful wife Tamara and my daughter Bethany for their support.

There has been an agreement in prayer of my prayer team, joining our faith in agreement, according to Matthew 18:19, with all who read this book and act on it against the evil spirits, demons, and ghosts who have attacked, afflicted. oppressed, tempted to sin, caused trouble, or any other things these spirits do to people. We join our faith with you to get rid of these spirits forever and for you to find peace in life and with God.

# Table of Contents

# Introduction

U sing the entertainment media in today's world as a ther-
mometer to gauge the interest of paranormal activity in our
society, it would appear it is a subject of great interest. On the television, there are any number of channels that you may frequent and
find stories of exorcism, haunted houses, evil spirits, and demon
possession. People are beginning to openly tell of paranormal activities over the television (including the exorcism or casting out of
devils) while others visit haunted places to find out if there really
are ghosts or evil spirits. Movies involving demon possession draw
big crowds. The big question is, "Are evil spirits, demons, devils,
and ghosts real, or just Hollywood stories? Is there an unseen world
around us that can touch us but we have no idea of its existence?
Can these spirits possess people, places, or things? Can they hurt us,
speak to us, haunt us, attack us and/or make us sick? Can we stop
them or do we just have to live with it if they oppress, attack, or

haunt us? In this book, we will be looking to the oldest, most trusted book on the planet to find the answers to these questions, the Bible.

Certainly, if they are real and there is an unseen world full of beings all around us, the more we can understand about that world, the better equipped we will be to deal with that world. Jesus spent quit a bit of time teaching on these beings. We will look into the scriptures to see what Jesus said about them, discover things about them, and learn how to deal with them. It is certain that this author does not know all there is to know about that world or those beings, but it is a start. This knowledge was not acquired in any other way but by the scriptures. There are some experiences mentioned, but they coincide with and came about as a result of scripture.

There is enough information, given in this book, to allow any one to understand what is going on in their lives and how to deal with such paranormal experiences. The information given in this book will mostly be derived from the King James Version of the Bible. The Book of Enoch, however, is also used to tell of origins of evil spirits, and personal experiences are used to manifest a truth the Bible teaches.

One goal of this book is that other saints who have knowledge on this subject, will come forth to share their wealth of information so who ever is afflicted, tormented, harassed, or fearful of such beings might know the truth and the truth set them free.

The public should know that ignorance of these beings is not bliss, but dangerous, even as ignorance of the presence of a rattle snake is not bliss, but dangerous. Many people want to be as the ostrich and hide their heads in the sand when it comes to evil spirits, demons, and/or ghosts. This is dangerous as it allows these spirits to attack and destroy with little to no resistance. Just ask all the people that are tormented by such spirits; and, yet do not have a clue what to do about it.

Young children are very perceptible to things in the spirit world. They can see and hear things most adults can't. After many years of ministry, the author has counseled with many children and their parents on this matter. Small children (at least some) see things and know things in the spirit world most grown-ups can neither see nor perceive. This needs to be known by parents so they won't discard what the child has experienced as a dream or imagination. Children are known to see apparitions, see things move about in their rooms, hear voices, have strange visitors, hear banging on the wall, hear footsteps, or even be attacked. Some children (adults too) come up with strange scratches, bumps, and bruises with no explanation for them. Some have bite marks but was never bitten by anything seen. It is true that sometimes, children make these things up, but that is not always the case with every child. Parents need to listen closely to their children to see what they have to say. Look in their eyes for truth, fear, and torment. Question them time and time again to see if they tell the same thing the same way. If they do, they are probably telling the truth. The children may even speak a knowledge that is beyond their age. There are children who have had such experiences that were three and four years old and yet they knew things like numbers, colors, and details that they are too young to know. They have had a spiritual experience, which means they knew it in their spirits even though their heads didn't know it. One child, a little over two years of age, told of seeing a spider-man that came to save him from an evil man who had entered his room. He said that an evil man came through the window but the "spider man" came and saved him. It was thought he might be speaking of the comic book "spider man" even though this child had never seen that show or comic book. However, for months after that event, you could question the child and he always came back with the same story; the parent tried to make him trip up on his details, but the child told the same thing, disagreeing with his dad when ever his dad told him it must be another way. While pondering on it one night, a scripture came to the councilor about a prophet in the Old Testament that saw a creature that had three pairs of wings, "…with twain he covered his feet, with twain he covered his face, and with twain he did fly," Isaiah 6:2. This creature was known as a Seraph. Notice with three pairs of wings and two feet, the Seraph had eight limbs like that of a spider. He could have easily been perceived as a spider man to a two year old. However, this two year old didn't know a spider had eight legs neither had he ever heard of a Seraph. That is, he didn't know it in the flesh, but he knew it in the spirit.

When my youngest child, Kyle, was eleven years old, he had a terrifying experience. One winter night, he was sleeping in the living room in a sleeping bag. We lived in a small three-bedroom house with a floor furnace located in the living room that heated the whole house. He wanted to sleep close to the furnace. It was not long after we had gone to bed when I heard a blood-curdling scream come from the living room area. It was Kyle. He was in his sleeping bag, totally terrified. This was one little boy that nothing scared; yet he was totally terrified. I asked him what happened and he said that something had dragged him out of his sleeping bag across the living room to the TV and was choking him. When it let him go, he was so scared he couldn't talk, so he crawled back to the sleeping bag until he calmed down enough to scream. He said he didn't know if he couldn't scream because he was so scared or if the thing had cut off his wind so he couldn't scream. I knew right away that some evil spirit had entered into my house and attacked my son. It made me mad. I screamed out, "How dare you come into my house and attack my son! You get out of this house, off this property, and don't you ever come back in Jesus' name!" Kyle refused to sleep in the living room after that, so he slept with his mother and me for a few days. It took a few days to assure him that I had taken care of the spirit and that it wouldn't be back. Nothing like that ever happened again. Most parents would have believed that the child was dreaming or made it up. I knew better. My son turned 25 in February of this year, and he still tells the story the same way he did back then. He didn't make it up. It was real enough for him to emphatically remember some 14 years later.

There is a cry for help coming from common-everyday people, who are intelligent and honest people. People, who have nothing to gain from telling of their harrowing experiences. You see, such activities occur more often then realized and to more people than acknowledged. Most people don't say anything because of the fear that family, friends, or society will think they are sick, going crazy, or lying. They themselves wonder if they are crazy. They endure their tortures day after day and night after night. They question: "Is this real?" "Am I going crazy?" "I must be dreaming!" "What is happening to me?" "Is there any help or hope for me?" They may go to doctors, psychiatrists, and even many ministers who are ignorant of the unseen world or of how to deal with its occupants. As a matter of fact, the general public, most ministers, and lay people know so little about how to deal with such phenomenon. There are a few, but they are not well known. That is why a book like this is needed; to give knowledge of these things to the common man so they can have an idea of what is going on and what to do about it. It is also needed so the clergy can assist their parishioners who are undergoing torment from these beings. Many churches pray about it, but very little help is realized. That is because Jesus didn't say pray about the devil, he said resist him and cast him out. It is our job to tend to the unclean spirits. Jesus didn't say we could pray and he would resist the devil for us or cast him out. That is our job. It is our responsibility for we have the authority of earth to do such. If there is no help, then they will live in terror, fear, and dread. Their life will simply be a nightmare.

There is however, help for them. There is a way out. God made a way through Jesus Christ. You can take charge of your own life if you will believe the truth. Jesus said, "… you shall know the truth, and the truth will make you free." This book presents to its readers the truth according to the Holy Scriptures so they can be free.

Indeed, there may be many of you that are experiencing paranormal activities in your home or in your life this very day. You may or may not have told people for fear of being misunderstood or not believed. God showed me people who wouldn't dare go to anyone for help for this matter, picking up this book with a gleam of hope in their eyes that maybe this is God's answer to their prayers. It is! If this is you, then this book is written for you, to help you to understand what is happening or happened to you and how to begin to deal with it. If you will believe this ancient manuscript, the Bible, and do what it says, it will set you free. His word brings knowledge and wisdom in such matters and how to deal with these spirits. May God Bless you as you read this book and open your eyes to its truth that you may take control of your life and stop the tormenting spirits that may be harassing you.

This is important for a person to understand. Just because a person is possessed or ministered to by an evil spirit doesn't mean the person is evil or sinful. It might be they don't know the truth on the subject. It might be that through ignorance the person opened a door for the spirit to harass them. It might be that a wondering spirit may have just decided to settle on them and they didn't know it or how to deal with it. It is no more a sin for an evil spirit to indwell a person than for a virus or bacteria to indwell a person's body. Even the holiest saint has to fight off evil spirits in one-way or another. If Jesus did, you will!

## The Book of Enoch

Most of the information in this book is taken out of the Bible; however, the most detailed account of the origin of evil spirits comes from the Books of Enoch (I Enoch or the Ethiopian Enoch and the 2 Enoch or Slavonic Enoch, which is also called the Book of the Secrets of Enoch). There has been controversy among theologians and Christians over the past several years as to whether the books of Enoch are scripture and whether they should be included in the holy cannon. The reason that it was not accepted was because Enoch wrote that the angels of God saw the daughters of men, that they were very beautiful, and came down to earth and married them. The offspring of these unions were great giants. However, as time goes by, there is more and more evidence indicating these writings are scripture inspired by God and should be included in the holy cannon. This author believes it to be scripture for the following reasons: (1) Genesis 6:1-4 tells the same story but not in as much detail as the book of Enoch. It says the sons of God saw the daughters of men that they were very fair and they made wives of them of whomever they chose. These sons of God are angels of God, as seen in Job 1:6. (2) Jesus, Himself made over 100 references to the teachings in the Books of Enoch in His teachings while on the Earth, (3) 2 Peter 2:4

is taken from the book of Enoch where it talks about the angels that sinned, (4) Jude 6 is also taken from the book of Enoch, and (5) Jude 14-15 quotes the book of Enoch. This would seem to indicate that the first church and Jesus accepted the book of Enoch as scripture. If it is quoted in the Bible and Jesus taught its principals, then it must be inspired of God.

# Part 1

# Knowing your enemy

# CHAPTER 1

# Do evil spirits exist?

Are there beings called unclean spirits, evil spirits, demons, and devils? This is a subject that you rarely, if ever, hear taught on or ministered on from the pulpit. I have never heard any teachings on spirits (but the Holy Spirit). Most people hurriedly read over the scriptures dealing with casting out of unclean spirits as though it isn't important or doesn't have anything to do with them. There are ministers out there who mention evil spirits, demons, and devils, but I have never heard anyone go into detail about what the scriptures teach on them. When reading about Jesus casting out evil spirits, readers pass over it much as we do a sentence that has a word in it we don't know. Jesus even took the time in scripture to talk about dealing with the spirits, but still there is a great lack of knowledge amongst believers and natural men on the subject. Let's look into the scriptures to better understand what they are, from where they came, what they do, and why. Later we will discuss how to deal with them.

When I began to have questions concerning the writings about evil spirits in the Bible, my first thought was that the people of that day were just superstitious and blamed sickness and disease on evil spirits. After all, if unclean spirits were real wouldn't our pastors, evangelist, and Sunday school teachers tell us of them? Most in traditional churches did not, and they certainly didn't tell us how to deal with these beings. So, unclean spirits must not be real. For a while, I believed when someone was healed in the Bible, the people of that day believed that an evil spirit came out. In other words, they blamed sickness and disease on evil spirits. However, I couldn't, in my wildest imagination, believe that Jesus was superstitious. He was the truth! Why didn't He tell them the truth about their superstitions? Why didn't He tell them there were no such things as evil spirits and devils/demons? Would not the Truth (Jesus) tell them the truth?

Matthew 4:24, "…and His fame went through out all Syria: and they brought unto Him all sick people that were taken with divers diseases and torments, and those that were possessed with devils, and those which were lunatic… This verse clearly identifies that the people who were sick were different from those who were possessed with devils.

Then another question came to me that I couldn't answer. If these unclean spirits were just superstitions, how were they able to talk to Jesus and how could He talk back? After all, superstitions, fairy tales, and myths were not real, so you couldn't talk to them. But, Jesus did, many times!

Mark 1:23, "And there was in their synagogue a man with an unclean spirit, and he cried out, saying, "Let us alone; what have we to do with Thee, Thou Jesus of Nazareth? Art Thou come to destroy us? I know Thee, who Thou art, the Holy One of God." In Mark 5:9 and Luke 8:30 Jesus asked the unclean spirit in the man of the Gadarenes what his name was. **He was talking to the unclean spirit**, not the man, for the unclean spirit answered and said, "My name is Legion, for we are many." The unclean spirit used the man's physical voice to speak to Jesus, showing an unclean spirit can speak through a human body. Then the **evil spirits** (all of them) **begged** Him not to cast them into the deep or abyss, but into the herd of swine feeding on the mountain. Jesus heard this in himself, in the spirit. They could not have all spoken through the man's voice at once. I believe this came in the form of thoughts to Jesus' mind. He heard them in the spirit. If you had been there, you would have heard, "My name is Legion for we are many," but you would not have heard them beg him to cast them into the herd of swine.

In this story, the unclean spirits exhibited emotions and char-acteristics like rage, anger, super human power, indecency, and violence. Just see how the man acted when these unclean spirits were in manifestation and you will see what spirits were in him. What ever emotion or feeling the unclean spirit was having, the man was experiencing also. With Jesus on the scene, these same spirits demonstrated fear, dread, and helplessness.

They also had wants or desires. They desired to be cast into the herd of swine rather than in the deep or abyss. People oppressed by or possessed by an unclean spirit or spirits exhibit the emotions and thoughts of the unclean spirit when the spirit has manifested itself in them.

It is possible for someone to have multiple spirits, and these spirits can manifest all at once. Remember Mary Magdalene had seven devils cast out of her in Luke 8:2. The mad man of Gadara also had a multiplicity of unclean spirits in him.

Unclean spirits can indwell animals also. It is through earthly bodies these spirits have a greater ability to express themselves on earth. They experience this world through the person's physical senses and can openly manifest their own person.

They also showed intelligence. They understood and obeyed Jesus as well as had a plan to petition Jesus to cast them into the herd of swine. They spoke His language. I believe they understand and speak all languages. In Mark 1: 34, Jesus ... "healed many that were sick of diverse diseases, and cast out many devils and suffered not the **devils to speak,** because they **knew** Him."

According to the book of Acts, there were unclean spirits that had to be dealt with after the death and resurrection of Jesus. In Acts

16:16, Paul was met by "a woman that was possessed with a spirit of divination (named python) who brought her owners much profit by her soothsaying (fortune telling)." Paul became grieved with her antics, turned around to her, and cast out the spirit by saying, "I command you in the name of Jesus Christ to come out of her." The spirit came out in the very same hour. It took an hour, but the spirit had to obey Paul as long as he stayed in faith. They will have to obey you too, if you will stay in faith. Sometimes, faith takes a little while to work; however, if we stay in faith and don't doubt, they have to come out. Phillip, in Acts 8:6-7, cast out evil spirits in Jesus' name at Samaria. In Acts 19:13-25, there were certain Vagabond Jews who were casting out unclean spirits in Jesus' name. They were neither Christ, apostle, or even Christian. They however, had faith in the name of Jesus even though they didn't know who He was.

Other scriptures like Matthew 7:22 states there will be many in the Day of Judgment that will say unto Jesus, "Lord, Lord, have we not prophesied in Thy name and in Thy name cast out devils." This indicates there will be people casting out unclean spirits until the Day of Judgment. It also indicates that people who are not serving Jesus can cast out unclean spirits. This won't get them into heaven, but they can do it while on the earth.

There are many more scriptures that speak of unclean spirits and devils/demons in the Old Testament and the New Testament. As a matter of fact the term "devils" is referred to 48 times in the Bible and the term "evil spirits" is referred to 10 times. If they do not exist, then why are they spoken so much of by holy men of God who were inspired by the Holy Ghost to give us the scriptures? Scriptures indicate that these beings are still here today and need to be dealt with. If they are real, then they are causing havoc today as they did then and we need to know how to stop them. This is what this book is about.

# CHAPTER 2

# The origin of evil spirits

B y a close study of the Bible, one can see that there are many types of spirits. The Bible speaks of unclean spirits, evil spirits, and demons/devils. Of course the Bible also speaks of good spirits as the Holy Spirit and angels. The Bible acknowledges the existence of ghosts, a different category of spirit that is on the earth.

Evil spirits and demons/devils all come under the heading of unclean spirits but are not the same things. For example, there is a group of animals called birds, but under that group come all the different birds with different characteristics like robins, blue jays, sparrows, etc. When Jesus classifies them as unclean spirits (Matthew 10:1, Mark 1:27, Mark 3:11, Luke 4:36, and Revelations 16:13 to mention just a few), He is talking about evil spirits and devils/demons as a whole. There is a difference between evil spirits and demons/devils even though man has to deal with them the same way. In Luke 10:19 Jesus said, "Behold, I give you power to tread on serpents and scorpions, and over all the power of the enemy; and nothing shall by any means hurt you." He divided them up into two categories except Jesus called them serpents and scorpions. It appears in scripture that demons and devils are two words used by the translators for the same type of spirit. From now on, demons and devils will be used interchangeable in this text.

There is not much revealed from the Bible about where evil spirits come from; however, the Book of Enoch is very explicit on the subject. The Book of Enoch is used in this chapter to discuss their origin. I will be backing up the account of Enoch with the Bible for those who want to see it in accepted scriptures.

The Book of Enoch Chapter 1-XXXVI section VI-XI,
VI. ...And it came to pass when the children of men had multiplied that in those days were born unto them beautiful and comely daughters. (2). And the angels, the children of the heaven, saw and lusted after them, and said to one another: Come, let us choose us wives from among the children of men and beget us children. (3). And Semjaza, who was their leader, said unto them: I fear, ye will not indeed agree to do this deed, and I alone shall have to pay the penalty of a great sin. (4). And they all answered him and said: Let us all swear

an oath, and all bind ourselves by mutual imprecations not to abandon this plan but to do this thing. (5). Then swear they all together and bound themselves by mutual imprecations. (6). And there were in all 200; who descended in the days of Jared on the summit of Mount Herman, because they had sworn and bound themselves by mutual imprecations upon it. VII. (1.) and all the others together with them took unto themselves wives, and each chose for himself one, and they began to go in unto them and to defile themselves with them… (2) And they became pregnant, and they bare great giants, whose height was three thousand Ells: (3) who consumed all the acquisitions of men. And when men could no longer sustain them, (4) the giants turned against them and devoured mankind. (5) And they began to sin against birds, and beasts, and reptiles, and fish, and to devour one another's flesh, and drink the blood. Chapter XV (8) and now the giants, who are produced from the spirits and flesh, shall be called evil spirits upon the earth, and on the earth shall be their dwelling. (9) Evil spirits have proceeded from their bodies; because they are born from men, and from the holy Watchers (angels) is their beginning and primal origin; they shall be evil spirits on earth, and evil spirits shall they be called. [(10) For the spirits of heaven (angels), in heaven shall be their dwelling, but as for the spirits of the earth which were born upon the earth, on the earth shall be their dwelling.]

(11) And the spirits of the giants (evil spirits) afflict, oppress, destroy, attack, do battle, and work destruction on the earth, and cause trouble; they take no food, but nevertheless hunger and thirst, and cause offenses (sins). XVI. (1) From the days of the slaughter and destruction and death of the giants, from the souls of whose flesh the spirits, having gone forth, shall destroy without incurring judgment-thus shall they destroy without incurring judgment – thus shall they destroy until the day of the consummation, the great judgment in which the age shall be consummated over the Watches and the godless, yea, shall be wholly consummated.

Here is a summary of Enoch's account of the time before and during the flood.

A group of the angels of God (called the sons of God in the Book of Enoch and in the King James Bible) see the daughters of men have become very beautiful, so much so, they lust after them. So, they make an agreement with each other to come down and marry these women. These women must be very beautiful because the angels know they will suffer a great punishment from God, however, they chose to do it anyway. Their punishment is spoken of in the New Testament in Jude 6. This scripture in Jude agrees with and prob-ably came out of The Book of Enoch. These women bare children to the angels, and these children are giants because they are born of angelic (spirit) men to natural women. It is the heavenly (spiritual) and earthly uniting. These giants began to eat all of the food man can grow, than they began to eat the animal's and men's flesh and drink their blood. They even turn and devour one another. The giants have a spirit but live in a giant natural body. When they die, they can't go to heaven for they are not from heaven, but their spirits have to remain on the earth for they are born on the earth. Their punishment is to stay here on earth and afflict, oppress, destroy, attack, do battle, and work destruction on the earth, and cause trouble. For those who would have trouble with the thought that God put on these evil spirits a curse to afflict, oppress, destroy, attack, and do battle against man, I remind you of Proverbs 16:4, "The Lord hath made all things for Himself, even the wicked for the day of evil." They also suffer hunger and thirst (which is God's just judgment for drinking men's blood and eating their flesh) but can never quench their thirst or satisfy their hunger. The Book of Enoch says they will do all of these things to man without suffering any punishment until the Day of Judgment.

This helps us to understand what the evil spirits were talking about when they asked Jesus if He had come to torment them before the time, Matthew 8:29. The time they were referring to was the day of consummation, the great judgment. That is why Jesus didn't cast them into the abyss because the command of God is that they will not suffer punishment for their transgression against man until the Day of Judgment. Many command the unclean spirits to go to the abyss when ministering deliverance. I do not because Jesus didn't.

I am not sure we can, as we don't have dominion or authority to decide what or who goes to the abyss. I am thinking He knows what He is doing and I am to follow His example. He allows them to go into the herd of swine. It is apparent Jesus did not want to torment them but neither was He going to let them torment or indwell man.

The Bible reads like this in Genesis 6:1-2, 4 and it came to pass when men began to multiply upon the face of the earth, and daughters were born unto them, that the sons of God saw the daughters of men that they were fair; and they took them wives of all which they choose. There were giants in the earth in those days; and also after that, when the sons of God came in unto the daughters of men, and they bare children unto them, the same became mighty men, which were of old, men of renown.

This is all I have found in the Bible about this incident, but you can see how it lines up with The Book of Enoch's account of the story. These giants were here before Noah's flood and were one main cause of the flood. The giants and their heavenly fathers had corrupted the whole earth except for Noah. Thus, God destroyed them with the flood.

Here is an interesting point concerning those days of Noah's time. In Matthew 24: 37-39, Jesus was teaching on the coming of the Son of Man. He said "But as the days of Noah were, so shall also the coming of the Son of Man be. For as in the days that were before the flood they were eating and drinking, marrying and giving in marriage, until the day that Noah entered into the ark. And knew not until the flood came and took them all away; so shall also the coming of the Son of Man be." Eating and drinking, marrying and giving in marriage have been around since the beginning of man. Why did Jesus pick Noah's time to, talk about, as a sign for the coming of the Son of Man? Why didn't He pick David's, or Solomon's, or Elijah's time period? Could it be speaking of something more undesirable as the daughters of men being given in marriage unto the sons of God (angels) and their children (the Giants) eating the flesh of animals and man and drinking their blood as is recorded in the Book of Enoch? I believe this was why Jesus picked Noah's day. It was to be a sign for believers to look for before He comes back. It might be a little hard to believe about the sons of God (angels) marrying women today, but maybe not when you consider that even now through modern technology men are searching for a union of the metaphysical (spiritual) world and science.

Revelations 12:4, "The dragon's tail drew a third of the stars of heaven and caused them to fall to the earth." Could these stars actually be angels that Satan will lure down in the last days to once again marry mortal women? If this happens, then the women will once again bear giants who will drink the blood of animals and man, which will be a sign of the coming of the Son of Man. This would fulfill the prophecy Jesus gave about the time of the coming of the

Son of Man. Some in witch covens and satanic cults have claimed to have sexual relations with Satan himself.

# CHAPTER 3

# Demons

There are no books, I know of, that tell us where demons origi-
nated. Some theologians think they are the spirits of men that
existed before Adam in what is called the pre-Adamite world. I want
to take scriptures from the Bible to explore this possibility. In doing
so, we will take scriptures you may have read many times dealing
with the subject of creation. Please take time to look at these scriptures again with an open mind.

Let's begin with the book of beginnings, the book of Genesis.
Genesis 1:1, "In the beginning God created the heavens and the
earth." Genesis 1:2, "and the earth was without form and void;
and darkness was upon the face of the deep." The Hebrew words
translated "was without form and void" are the words "hayah
tohuw bohum." Proper translation of these words is "hayah" (to be,
become, come about, happen), "tohuw" (formlessness, confusion,

unreality, emptiness), and "bohum" (emptiness, void, waste). The word "hayah" is a verb in the qal pattern. The qal verb pattern is the most frequently used verb pattern in the Bible. Some examples of this verb pattern are: "he sat," "he went," "he ate," and "he read." All of these are in the past tense. Genesis 1:1 should read the earth **became** formless, empty, void, and waste. This translation indicates that the earth was not created that way in Genesis 1:1, but rather, became that way before Genesis 1:2. It is hard to imagine that a perfect being like God would create anything that is formless, void, waste, or empty. Everything else He created He created in perfection. Why not the earth?

Before we begin, understand this, the scriptures were not originally written in chapter and verse. They were divided into chapter and verse at the discretion of the translators. Genesis 1 should end on chapter 2:3. Chapter 2 should begin with verse 4, which states "These are the generations of the heavens and the earth when they were created." This is where the heavens, the earth, and its inhabitants actually begin. If you look closely and examine Genesis 1 and Genesis 2 it is obvious they are not talking about the same creation. Genesis 2 is describing the creation of what is known as the pre-Adamite world, where Genesis 1 is talking about the re-creation of that earth and man after a flood occurred which destroyed it somewhere between Genesis 1:1 and Genesis 1:2. Calling the world of Genesis 2 the pre-Adamite world is incorrect; because the man created first in this world was the first Adam. Let's call this world "the world of the first Adam."

If you study Genesis closely, there are many indications of man existing before Genesis 1:3 or 1:26. For instance in Genesis 1:28 God tells Adam and Eve to "Be fruitful, multiply, replenish, and subdue the earth." The only way you can "replenish" something is if there was something there before, indicating that God wanted this Adam to replenish the earth with man once again. We are going to see how Genesis 1:2-31 is a **re-creation** of the earth that was **first created** in Genesis 2:4-25.

Genesis 2:4, "These are the generations of the heavens and the earth when they were created, in the day when the Lord God made the earth and the heavens." Many believe this to be a recap of what happened in Genesis chapter 1. You will see it is not. This is the very first time God made the heavens, the earth, and man. Let's compare Genesis 1 and Genesis 2 looking for evidence of two different events. Play close attention to the bold words.

There is a difference in order of the creation of man and plant life between the two chapters of Genesis. Genesis 2 states that God had not brought forth plants because there was not a man to till the ground. Genesis 2:5, "…and every plant of the field **before** it was in the earth, and every herb of the field **before** it grew: for the Lord God had not caused it to rain upon the earth, and there **was not** a man to till the ground." One reason God had not brought forth the plants in Genesis 2:5 is because there was not a man to till the ground. God wanted a man to be able to till the ground before he was going to create the plants, trees, etc. Genesis 2:7, "…and the Lord God formed man of the dust of the ground, and breathed into his nostrils the breath of life; and man became a living soul." You will see later on in the chapter this to be just man and not woman. After God creates Adam, He creates the Garden of Eden to put the man He has already formed in [Genesis 2: 8, "and the Lord God planted a garden eastward in Eden; and there He put the man **whom He had formed** (past tense)"]. Genesis 2:9 indicates God made the trees **after the creation of man** in order to put them in the Garden of Eden.

Compare this with Genesis 1: 12-13 which says on the third day, "God, brought forth grass and herb yielding seed after its kind, and the tree yielding fruit, whose seed was in itself, after its kind." Then on the sixth day, Genesis 1:26, "Let us make man in Our image, after Our likeness: and let them have dominion over the fish of the sea, and over the fowl of the air, and over the cattle, and over the earth, and over everything that creepeth upon the earth." It is clear here that man was created after God brought forth plants. The chronological order of Genesis 1 is the plants being created on the third day, the fish of the sea and fowls of the air on the fifth day, and the land animals and creeping things right before man, on the sixth day.

In contradiction to Genesis 1, Genesis 2:18-20 shows Adam being created first, then the plants, and the animals sometime after wards. Genesis 2: 18-20, "and the Lord God said **it is not good for**

**the man to be alone; I will make him a help meet for him. And out of the ground the Lord God formed every beast of the field, and every fowl of the air;** (trying to find a help meet for him) and brought them unto Adam to see what he would call them: and whatsoever Adam called every living creature, that was the name there of. And Adam gave names to all cattle, and to the fowls of the air and to every beast of the field; **but for Adam there was not found a help meet for him.**" In Genesis 2 account, God created man first, saw that it was not good for the man to be alone, so He created all the animals for a help meet, but saw there was still no help meet for Adam. So He created a woman from Adams rib. Genesis 2:21-22, "And the Lord God caused a deep sleep to fall upon Adam, and he slept: and He took one of his ribs (tsela), and closed up the flesh instead thereof; and the rib (tsela) which the Lord God had taken from man, made He a woman, and brought her unto the man."

The translators here used the word "rib" for the Hebrew word "tsela." This word also has the meaning of an inner chamber or **cell**. Could it be that God cloned a woman out of Adam by taking a cell and changing the chromosomes to xx rather than xy? Perhaps this cell came out of the marrow in his rib? The translators would have never chosen the word "cell" to translate the word "rib" as they did not have the knowledge of cells or DNA that is known today. They would have thought a cell was something like a jail.

Once again let's compare the chronological order of the two chapters. Genesis 1 has the plants being brought forth first on the third day. The fish of the sea and the fowls of the air are brought forth on the fifth day. The land animals and creeping things are brought forth on the sixth day first and then Adam and Eve were brought forth together on the sixth day. In Genesis 2, man is brought forth first. After man is here, God brings forth the trees and plants and creates the Garden of Eden to put Adam in, whom He has already created. Adam is alone and God sees it is not good, so then God creates the beast of the fields (animals and insects) and brings them to Adam as a helpmeet. Adam names them, but still there is no helpmeet for him. Then, God takes one of Adams ribs (tsela) and creates women. This is a completely different order of events than in Genesis 1, hence two different earths and two different Adams, and two different worlds. This first creation could very possibly be the origin of the demon spirits spoken of in the Bible.

It is believed Lucifer led the first Adam's world in rebellion against God (much as he is trying to do today) and God destroyed it with a flood. I use the name Lucifer because there is an evil spirit or demon by the name Satan. Lucifer is a fallen angel. These beings were never angels.

This flood spoken of in the last paragraph is not Noah's flood, but a flood that happened a long time before Noah's day. Geology supports the two-flood theory. By studying rock layers and forma-tions, geologists have found evidence of two great deluges in the history of the earth. One is Noah's flood but one is before Noah. 2 Peter 3:5-6 gives an account of this flood. It says, " For this they are willingly ignorant of, that by the word of God the heavens were of old, and the earth standing in the water and out of the water: whereby the world that then was, being overflowed with water, perished." This is not talking about Noah's flood because the whole world is not destroyed in Noah's day thanks to Noah. This world is completely destroyed by water leaving the earth without form, waste, empty, and void. It apparently had an effect on the landscape as well as destroying all life.

Between these two worlds, could have been the period of the ice age. After all, if there is no light in Genesis 1, then there is probably not much heat. Genesis 1 says water covered the face of the earth, so if you have water with little heat, you wind up with ice. I believe the Bible does not contradict true science and true science does not contradict the Bible. It is just scientific theory that contradicts the Bible.

It is possible, that the spirits of these inhabitants (men) destroyed by the flood are the demons mentioned in the Bible and in our world today. The Book of Enoch says that which is born of the earth must remain on the earth. These men were born on the earth so if the Book of Enoch is scripture, then their spirits must be on the earth somewhere. There is, however, no scripture (I have found) to back this up.

Wherever demons came from, they are not the same as the evil spirits. The Book of Enoch tells how the angels of God saw the daughters of men and how fair they were so they came to earth and co-inhabited with them. It also tells how these angels taught men

41

to sin and one of the sins they taught them was witchcraft. I don't know a lot about witchcraft except that it uses chants, incantations, and potions to control and order these demon spirits to do things. This being true, then demons had to be here before the giants, whom we have already discovered, became evil spirits upon their demise during Noah's time. The demons had to have already been here in order for the Angels to teach their wives how to control them.

# CHAPTER 4

# Ghosts

The Bible doesn't have a lot to say about the subject of ghosts, except to acknowledge their existence. Luke 24:36-37, "and as they thus spoke, Jesus stood in the midst of them, and saith unto them, "peace be unto you." But they were terrified and affrighted, and supposed that they had seen a spirit (ghost)." Matthew 14:26, "and when the disciples saw Him (Jesus) walking on the sea, they were troubled, saying, "it is a spirit (the New King James Bible actually says ghost); and they cried out for fear."

Through the scriptures we can see ghosts are the spirits of human beings that have died. Genesis 25:8, "Then Abraham gave up the ghost, and died in a good old age." Genesis 25:17, "...and he gave up the ghost and died; and was gathered unto his people." Genesis 35:29, "and Isaac gave up the ghost, and died, and was gathered to his people." Matthew 27:50, "Jesus, when He had cried again with a loud voice, yielded up the ghost." These all tell what happens at the death of men, the spirit leaves and the body dies. The Bible calls these spirits "ghosts."

In Luke 24:39, "...handle Me and see; for a spirit (ghost) hath not flesh and bones, as you see Me have." Jesus had to prove to His disciples, after His resurrection, He wasn't a ghost. If Jesus, who is the Truth, had to prove to the disciples that He wasn't a ghost or spirit, but didn't tell them there were no such things as ghost, then He would be allowing them to believe something that wasn't true. Jesus didn't tell them there were no such things; He told them He wasn't one. That was a good indication there were ghosts. However, He did not tell how to deal with these entities, unless they can be dealt with as the demons and evil spirits.

In confronting ghosts, I have suggested you treat it as though it were a demon or evil spirit. It has been said, by some who have dealt with this type of spirit, if you can convince them they are dead; they will leave this realm and depart to the realm in which they are supposed to be. I have also heard that some won't leave because they know or are afraid they will go to hell." If this is so, they still don't have the right to abide in your house or property. You have the authority over that.

# CHAPTER 5

# How evil spirits and demons operate?

1 Peter 5:8-9, "Be vigilant, be sober; because your adversary the devil, (this is not necessarily talking about Lucifer, whom we know as Satan, but any unclean spirit) as a roaring lion, walketh about, seeking whom he may devour; whom resist steadfast in the faith, knowing that the same afflictions (remember the evil spirits are to afflict men) are accomplished in your brethren who are in the world." This agrees with what Jesus said about unclean spirits, that they roam about looking for a place of rest. Peter says your adversary (the devil) walks about as a roaring lion seeking whom he may devour. In the animal world, all predators, including the lion, choose the weakest, frailest, and slowest members of a herd to attack. It is often the young, old, or those who are weakened by accident or disease. These spirits are like that, in that they attack people who

are spiritually, mentally, and even emotionally and perhaps physically (because of an accident or illness) weak. This is especially true of babies and small children. In ministering deliverance for many years, many of the demons and evil spirits I dealt with entered the person when they were very young. That is why it is important for parents to stay strong in God and stand watch over their young.

How do they take control of a man's life? How do they get in? Luke 11:21-23, Jesus said, "When a strong man armed keepeth his palace (life, body, or mind), his goods are in peace: but when a stronger than he cometh upon him and overcometh him, he taketh from him all his armor where in he trusted, and divideth his spoils." The strong man can be the man's spirit who actually lives in that body or an unclean spirit that has overcome the man's spirit and taken up residence in his life, body, mind, and/or soul. When the unclean spirit comes to the man to possess his/her life (body, soul, mind, etc.) there will be a conflict between the man's spirit and the unclean spirit. Depending on the strength of the man's spirit and the unclean spirit, the battle may take a while; however, if the man will stay in faith and not give up, the unclean spirit will have to leave. I have fought evil spirits trying to attack me for as much as three days. If the man's spirit is weaker than the unclean spirit, the unclean spirit will enter into his/her life and he will began to exhibit the characteristics of the spirit that over took him. If it is a spirit of murder, at the very least, he/she will have thoughts of murder. This is why you hear murderers confess that the devil told them to do it or a voice talks to them telling them to do it. They are probably not lying. However, they don't have to yield to the voice or the devil. They can resist it. If it is a spirit of rebellion, he/she will exhibit characteristics of rebellion, and so on. The mad man of Gadara exhibits characteristics of self-mutilation, indecency, anger, rage, super human strength, and uncleanness. There are probably many other characteristics that are not mentioned such as insanity, hatred, fear, and who knows what else as he had many spirits in him.

If there is someone reading this book that hears these voices or has these thoughts, read this book carefully and act on it. This can help you from ruining your life and taking an innocent life. Tell this spirit to get out of your life and leave you alone forever.

Unclean spirits can come in through several openings. Being drunk and/or high on drugs makes someone very susceptible to these spirits as the senses are numbed and the mental alertness and strength wane. Dabbling in the occult as Satanism, witchcraft, séances, astrology, cultic games, going to palm readers, tarot card readers, astroprojection, etc will also open the door to demon spirits of witchcraft. When spirits of witchcraft manifest through a person, they often will act like a serpent with a slithering tongue. They will slide their tongue in and out of their mouth like a serpent does. Some have even fallen in the floor and squirmed like a snake on its belly. It has been said that certain types of music, rhythm and beats, open a person up to demon possession. Songs of death, murder, suicide, and just general ungodliness are said to open these doors. Evil spirits coming out of people have said they came in through the music the person was listening too. I personally have never come across that but I don't doubt its truth. If David's music could drive off the evil spirit ministering to Saul in 1 Samuel 16:23, there is no reason not to believe that a different type of music would draw them.

Unclean spirits are roaming the earth this very moment, trying to find someone weak enough or naïve enough to inhabit. Peter teaches however, that we can resist them in faith. We don't have to yield to their whims. We may not win the battle right away, but as we struggle against the sin or spirit, we will grow strong enough to overcome the spirit or sin one day. As a person struggles against the unclean spirit, the person gets stronger.

When it is about the time for the person to overcome the unclean spirit, there could possibly be an increase in intensity and number of manifestations of the unclean spirits. Like a final battle in a war, the side losing puts up its last stand with all they have to win. These spirits will do the same thing with all kinds of manifestations. Knowing this can bring encouragement and hope if you are the one fighting against the devil. This is not only true if you are seeking deliverance for yourself, but also true when ministering deliverance to others. In many of the deliverances Jesus ministered, the spirits were in strong manifestation when they came out. An example is Mark 9:17-26 in which Jesus cast an unclean spirit out of a boy, but before the spirit came out, it cried with a loud voice and tore the young man severely. This scripture has a lot of information in it that will help you if you will read it and study it closely.

Words play an important part in the operation of these spirits as well as in the way man has to defend himself from these same spirits. In Matthew 12:43-44 and Luke 11:24-26, Jesus says, "When the unclean spirit is gone out of a man, he walketh through dry places seeking rest, and findeth none, **he saith,** (notice the spirit demonstrates communication skills, intelligence, and the ability to plan ahead) I will return unto my house whence I came out." This shows how unclean spirits say something before they do it. We do the same thing. If we want to wash the car, we say to ourselves, "I am going to go wash the car." We say it before we do it. We do that for everything we do. These spirits do the same things. It is a spiritual law that these spirits operate on, and man also operates on it.

Sometimes when we think evil thoughts like, "I am going to take that money," the thought wasn't ours but the words of the evil spirit that has come upon us or is ministering to us. That doesn't mean we are possessed any more than Jesus was possessed when the devil tempted Him in the wilderness. The wicked thought was planted in our heads. However, if we continue to listen, without a response as Jesus made, or if we submit to the devil's evil thoughts and feelings (desires), or if we allow the words to dwell in our thoughts, the thoughts can enter into our hearts and we can become possessed by this demon even as Judas Iscariot became possessed at the last supper. Even the most holy saint you can think of has had thoughts that were repugnant to him/her. Even though they were in their head, the thought wasn't theirs. It didn't come from their heart. The enemy has won many a battle by telling the saint, "You thought it. You might as well do it." That is not so. Jesus had the thought to turn the stone into bread, but He didn't accept the thought.

He spoke the written word to combat thoughts and temptations. He said, "It is written, man shall not live by bread alone but by every word that proceeds from the mouth of God." It maybe the enemy's thought or words, but you don't have to accept it. God told Joshua, in Joshua 1:8, that he was not to let the word of God depart from his mouth. That means when he speaks, it should always be the word of God. These unclean spirits will try to put other words in our mouth like "turn the stone into bread." Jesus didn't let the word leave His mouth and the word of the devil enter into it. **A word can't come out of your mouth unless it is in there first.** In order for Jesus to have said, "Ok, I'll turn the stone into bread," the words, "man shall not live by bread alone but by every word that proceedeth from the mouth of God" would have had to not be in His mouth. Your mouth speaks whatever is in it. Jesus had the word in His mouth and that is what came out during the temptation.

These unclean spirits can come upon us at anytime. Whether they gain something over us or not, will depend on whether we receive the thought or not. They know we receive the thought if we act on it or say it. They know for sure we don't accept that thought if we speak the word, as Jesus did when He said, "It is written, man shall not live by bread alone, but by every word of God," Luke 4:4. The very fact that Jesus spoke the words out loud indicates to me that neither these unclean spirits nor Satan himself can read our thoughts. We must **speak** scripture, out loud, to defeat every unclean spirit. I was casting an evil spirit out of a lady once and I told it, "The word says you have to come out." It retorted back at me, "No it doesn't either." I said, "That is correct, but it gives me authority over you and you have to come out because I told you too." It didn't say anything else, it just came out. That is why the word (Bible) is called the sword of the spirit in Ephesians Ch. 6. Sometimes people are overcome because they don't say back, "No I'm not either, the word says..." or "No your not, the word says!"

Going back to the scriptures in Matthew 12 and Luke 11, after the unclean spirit says, "I will return unto the house from whence I came, And when he cometh he findeth it swept, and garnished. And then goeth he, and taketh to him seven other spirits that are more wicked then himself, and they enter in and dwell there: and the last state of that man is worse than the first." The first thing from this scripture we notice about the unclean spirit (remember that includes evil spirits and demons) is they don't necessarily stay in or on a person all the time. They come and go. Matthew 17:14-18 and Mark 5:1-13 both are stories about demon-possessed people who were not always under the control of the demon. In Matthew 17, the spirit often came upon the boy throwing him in the fire and in the water. This shows the unclean spirit was not always on him or it wouldn't

51

often come on him. In Mark 5 the man must have been in his right mind sometimes or the people would have never been able to put chains and fetters on him for him to "pluck asunder and break in pieces" when the unclean spirit was on him.

Here is how unclean spirits operate, according to what Jesus said in Matthew 12:43-44 and Luke 11:24-26. When unclean spirits come out of a man they go through dry places seeking rest. It is doubtful they can find rest anywhere as that is the curse on them for their sin against God. What does He mean by a "dry place?" Remember we are talking about spirits, so a dry place to a spirit is not a physical desert, but rather a spiritual one. The Bible likens the word of God and the Holy Spirit to water in John 7:38 and Ephesians 5:26. A dry place would be a place where very little, if any, of the word of God is present. This could be in some one's life or heart, or a place where sin abounds, or in someone who does not have the word (which is the sword that defeats these unclean spirits). That is why it is so important to keep the word of God in our hearts by reading it, meditating on it, and speaking it. When they do not find a place of rest, they go back to the person from whom they came out and find the house (his body or life) swept and garnished (neat, clean, and normal).

There is a misunderstanding of this scripture in the body of Christ. Because the scripture says in Matthew 12: 44, when the unclean spirit comes back to the house from which he left, "he findeth it empty, swept, and garnished," many think that being empty is the reason the unclean spirit can come back in. This is not what Jesus is saying. What He is saying is when the unclean spirit is gone, the man's life straightens out (becomes swept and garnished) and he is no longer under this unclean spirit's spell. He is normal again. He is getting or gotten his life back together. When the spirit comes back and brings seven worse spirits with him, the unclean spirit finds the man normal and his life straightened out and enters in and brings the seven worse spirits with him. The man becomes worse then he was before. That is why the mad man of the Gadarene's (Mark 5:1-13) had a legion of demons. The spirit left and kept bringing back more demons every time. The good news here is if the man becomes spiritually strong enough to keep the unclean spirit out, when the unclean spirit comes back, the man keeps him and his buddies out. That is why when ministering deliverance, it is important to either command the unclean spirit to never come back and/or teach the man the word of God so that he grows strong enough on his own to keep the unclean spirit out.

These spirits have subjected everyone to attacks. Whether you believe in them or not, it doesn't matter, you have been and will be attacked by them. I have ministered deliverance to dozens of people who had unclean spirits in them or on them but were unaware of it until they got in a situation where the unclean spirit was made to manifest itself. One young man asked me what kept him from having an evil spirit in him. I answered nothing. He asked me to find out. It turned out he had an unclean spirit called Satan in him at the very time he was asking me the question. I made the spirit manifest, and when he did; I got his name, and then cast him out. In the next chapter, we are going to discover why Jesus could cast out these unclean spirits and why you can get them out of your life too.

# Part II

# How to deal with them

# CHAPTER 6

# Man has dominion and authority over the earth

If you were to ask most people today how Jesus did the miracles He did while on earth, most would say because He was the Son of God. They forget Philippians 2:7-8 which says, " …but made Himself of no reputation, and took upon Himself the form of a servant, and was made in likeness of men: and being found in fashion as a man, humbled Himself and became obedient unto death, even the death of the cross." This scripture teaches Jesus stripped Himself of all rights and privileges as being the Son of God to become a man. If Jesus had any special power inherent in Him because He was the Son of God, He would not qualify as a natural man so would not be able to pay the price for man's sin. A perfect man has to die for the imperfect men and take the imperfect men's place in judgment. The Bible teaches Jesus was tempted in all points even as we are tempted, yet He sinned not. Jesus calls Himself, many times, the Son of Man (Adam). Therefore, the miracles He did He did as being a Son of Adam (man) and not the Son of God. We should be able to see this as Mark 6:5 states He **could not do any mighty works** in Nazareth except for laying His hands on a few sick folks and healing them. If Jesus did His works because of some power in Him as being the Son of God then He would have been able to heal anyone He wanted too. But, He <u>couldn't</u> heal these folks in Nazareth. It doesn't say He wouldn't, it says He <u>couldn't</u>.

We also need to remember that Jesus taught us in Mark 9:23, "… all things are possible to he that believeth." The "he" in here means any man (male and female). Jesus believes this and He is a man. If we are really going to believe the Bible and Jesus, then we must believe all things are possible to the man who believes. Casting out unclean spirits, killing the fig tree, walking on water, turning the water into wine, and healing the sick, cleansing the lepers, and raising the dead He did because He was a man who believed God rather than because He was the Son of God.

How did He do these miracles and how did He know how too if He didn't do it because He was the Son of God? He gives us a hint in Mark 11:23-24. Jesus had just finished cursing a fig tree and it died. His disciples were amazed at how fast the fig tree had died. Jesus told them **if they had faith in God, they could do this and they could command a mountain to be removed and cast into the sea,** and if they believed it in their heart, without doubting, the mountain would obey them. He didn't tell them if they were the Sons of God, they could do this. He said if **they had faith in God**. If we, as men, have faith, we can do these things too. Jesus said so. John 14:12, "Verily, verily, I say unto you, he that believeth on Me, the works that I do shall he do also; and greater works than these shall he do; because I go unto My Father." Remember, John 1:1-3 says Jesus is the word of God, so to believe in Jesus is to believe in the word of God. The works Jesus did, He did because He believed the word of God.

In order to believe God, Jesus had to know what God said. What did God say that Jesus believed that allowed Him to curse the fig tree, walk on water, raise the dead, turn the water into wine, cause the disciples to catch a boat sinking load of fish, and feed five thousand with just a few fish and 5 loaves of bread? What word did He believe? If we know, we can believe the same word and do the works that he did.

To find out, we have to once again go back to Genesis Chapter 1:26, " ...let Us make man in Our image, after Our likeness: and let **them** have dominion over the fish of the sea, the fowl of the air, and over the cattle, **and over all the earth**, and over ever creeping thing that creepeth upon the earth." From the beginning of the second Adam, God gave man dominion over the fish of the sea, the fowl of the air, and over the cattle, and **over all the earth,** and over every creeping thing. Jesus believed because He was a man He had authority over all the earth. He used this authority to still storms, calm seas, curse a fig tree, walk on water, cast out demons, feed thousands with a little food, etc. He told the Pharisees the Son of **Man** (not God) even had the power on earth to forgive sins. If you are man (male or female), you also have been given the authority over the earth and all the things Genesis 1:26-27 says you have authority over. That includes evil spirits and demons on the earth. Jesus said (Luke 17:6), "If you have faith, as a grain of mustard seed, ye might say unto this sycamine tree, be thou plucked up by the root, and be thou planted in the sea; and it should obey you." He was teaching them to use the authority given to them as being men. To prove this authority was given to man and not just Jesus'. Let's look and see if there was anyone else who did miracles because of the authority given to man through Adam.

In Joshua 10:12, the children of Israel were in a fight against the Amorites. "Joshua, in the sight of Israel, spoke to the sun saying, "Sun, stand thou still upon Gibeon; and thou moon, in the valley of Ajalon."" The sun and the moon obeyed Joshua's command for about a whole day. This allowed Israel to win this battle. How could Joshua have done such a miraculous thing? He, too, believed God gave man (including him) authority upon the earth. Remember God's orders to Joshua through Moses was to "meditate the book of the law day and night that he might make his way prosperous and have good success" (Joshua 1:8). Genesis 1:26-27 where God told man to have dominion and authority over the earth was in the book of the law. Joshua saw he had authority to speak to the sun and moon from the book of the law. Others using this authority were Moses, when he split the red sea (Exodus 14:14-28), Elijah, when he split the Jordan River (2 Kings 2:8), Elisha, when he smote Israel's enemies with blindness (2 Kings 6:8-18), Elijah, when he called fire down from heaven to consume a captain with fifty men (2 Kings 1:9-12). Elijah also stopped the rain in Israel for many years and then made it rain again. Isaiah the prophet brought the sundial back 10 degrees, as a sign to King Hezekiah the word of the Lord would come to pass (2 Kings 20:1-11). Elisha caused an iron axe head to float like wood in water (2 Kings 6:5-7). The fire had no effect on the three Hebrew children (Daniel 3:10-28).

Obviously Jesus had the power and authority to cast out unclean spirits, but what about common man? In Luke 9:1, Jesus gave His apostles power over all devils. In Luke 10:17, Jesus gave 70 disciples power over devils in which, "they came back to Him rejoicing saying Master, even the devils are subject unto us through Your name." In Acts 8: 6-7, "And the people with one accord gave heed unto the things which Phillip spake, hearing and seeing the miracles which he did. For unclean spirits, crying with loud voice came out of many that were possessed with them…" Phillip was an evangelist, not an apostle or the Christ, yet he cast out devils. You don't have to be an apostle or the Christ to cast them out. In Mark 9:38, John caught a man casting out devils and John forbade him because he was not with them. Jesus said, "Forbid him not." This shows that Jesus was not the only one who cast out unclean spirits.

You do have to believe for as Mark 16:17 says, "...these signs shall follow them that believe, in my name shall they cast out devils..." In Acts 19:13-25, (this being also after the death and resurrection of Christ) "there were certain vagabond Jews who were casting evil spirits out of men by saying "we adjure you by Jesus whom Paul preaches to come out of him." These men apparently had success. Once again they were neither Christ, apostle, or even Christian. However, they must have had faith in Jesus' name. It goes on to say there were 7 sons of a man named Sceva who was a Jew and a high priest. These 7 men tried to cast out an evil spirit by saying the same thing the vagabond Jews were saying, ("we adjure you in the name of Jesus that Paul preaches to come out of him"). **The evil spirit spoke and said to them "Jesus I know and Paul I know but who are you?"** "He then (the evil spirit through the man) jumped on them and beat them and caused them to run out of the house naked, beaten, and bruised." One demon-possessed man was more than the 7-sons of Sceva could handle. This showed that a person under the control of an evil spirit would do what the evil spirit desires. He would have even killed them had they not been able to flee. I have heard it said they got beat up because they weren't Christians and had no right to use the name of Jesus. I disagreed with this assessment. The vagabond Jews (not Christians) were casting out devils by the same method but there was no report they ever were jumped on. There have been born-again, spirit-filled Christians (myself included) that have been jumped on by individuals when casting out unclean spirits.

All of this is important to know in order to be free from the tormenting spirits that are harassing you or a loved one. Man must realize that he/she has a God given right to take authority and dominion over unclean spirits and demons. Man was born with that authority. Nowhere in the Bible has that authority ever been taken away from man. It never passed away. Only a hand full of men have known this, but it is nonetheless true. These spirits are on the earth, but man is given dominion **over the earth**. Jesus said in Matthew 18:18 that, "Whatever you bind (don't allow to happen or to go forward) on earth will be bound in heaven and whatever you loose (allow to happen or to go forward) on earth will be loosed in heaven." These spirits have been allowed to torment, harass, afflict, tempt, and stay in our lives. Exercise authority over them and tell them to leave and not to come back. Do it in faith and heaven will back you up. Jesus said so. They will be bound where they can't minister. They will intimidate as long as they are allowed, but when a man takes his/her stand against them they must stop.

CHAPTER 7

# Power in the Name of Jesus

A cts 4:12, "Neither is there salvation in any other: for there is none other name under heaven given among men, whereby we must be saved." I want you to be clear on this matter, we do not fight these beings in our own name. We must use the name of Jesus against them. Mark 16:17, "And these signs shall follow them that believe; in My name shall they cast out devils." If we are going to war against these beings, our secret weapon is the name "Jesus." We must use it liberally when **commanding them**. The Bible says in Philippians 2:9-11, "Wherefore God also hath highly exalted Him, and given Him a name which is above every name: that at the name of Jesus every knee should bow, of **things (beings)** in heaven, **things (beings)** on the earth, and **things (beings)** under the earth; and that every tongue should confess that Jesus Christ is Lord, to the glory of

God the Father." These evil spirits and demons have names. We have read in the Bible of one spirit whose name was Legion. I have often made the spirits tell me their name. There have been such names as Argon, Satan, The Devil, and Destruction. There are others whose names are fear, hate, lust, perversion, witchcraft, and such like. But no matter what name they may have, they are all subject to the name of Jesus. Whether they come from heaven, the earth, or under the earth; the name of Jesus reigns supreme. All that we do, we are to do in the name of Jesus (Colossians 3:17). I have had spirits to tell me I was too weak to cast them out. I simply said, "That maybe true, but I don't come in my name, I come in the name of Jesus against you, and He is strong enough to cast you out." I depend upon that name to do the job. That unclean spirit has to bow its knee to that name.

Always use the name of Jesus when dealing with these spirits. There is no other name given to us whereby we must be saved. We must depend on that name. Jesus said in Matthew 28:18, "All power is given unto me in heaven and in earth," and then commanded the apostles to go forth in His name. He was saying He had the authority and power in heaven and in earth, and then delegated that authority to the believers. He commanded the apostles to go forth and to teach people to observe everything He had commanded them. That means if they were commanded to heal the sick, cleanse the lepers, cast out demons, and raise the dead, so should the believers. Believers are to do everything He commanded the apostles to do. Some say that only the apostles had the power to heal the sick and perform miracles. They either haven't read or don't believe Matthew 28:20 which says, "Teaching them to observe **all things** whatsoever I have commanded you." We believe and confess and preach the last part of that verse where He says, "and lo, I am with you always..." why don't we believe the first part that we are to do all things the apostles did? Jesus said in John 14:12, "Verily, verily, I say unto you, he that believeth on Me, the works that I do shall he do also; and greater works than these shall he do; because I go unto My Father." If we believe on Jesus, we ought to be doing the same works He did. Jesus said we could. Do we believe what He said? If we do, then we can cast the devil right out of our lives.

**We have to do it**; His power will back us up. It is according to our faith. If we have 100% faith, we can do anything. If we have 60% faith, we can do a lot. If we have 30% faith, we can do a few minor things. However, through meditation and speaking the word, we can acquire 100% faith (Mark 4 & Ephesians 4:15). We can have faith to move mountains. It is made available to us if we are willing to do what Jesus said to acquire that kind of faith. In Matthew 17:14-21, a story is told about a young boy who is possessed of a devil. The disciples couldn't get the spirit out. They ask Jesus why. He said, "Because of your unbelief;" but He says, "This kind goeth not out but by prayer and fasting." He was not talking about the demon. He was talking about that kind of faith. It goeth not out but by prayer and fasting. Every demon is subject to the name of Jesus. We, however, have to be at the level of faith to get them out. Jesus said this kind of faith cometh by prayer and fasting. In your situation, you may have to fast and pray and seek God, but Jesus said in Matthew 7:7, "Ask, and it shall be given unto you, seek, and ye shall find, knock, and the door shall be opened unto you." If you seek God for deliverance, He will grant it to you. Not every spirit is that strong. This one was, but even this one had to submit to the Man who was strong in faith.

Are you strong in faith? If the answer is no, fast and pray and read God's word until you become strong in faith. Remember, however, my faith is joined with yours in your battle against whatever spirit is attacking you and together our strength and faith is more than the spirit can handle. Speak to it in Jesus' name and tell it to get out of your life now, and leave you alone forever, and to never come back. My faith will join with you, and it shall be done.

How are these powers made available to us? Ephesians 1:19-23, "What is the exceeding greatness of His power **to us-ward who believe,** according to the working of His mighty power, which He wrought in Christ, when He raised Him from the dead, and set Him at His own right hand in the heavenly places, far above all principality, and power, and might, and dominion, and every name that is named, not only in this world, but also in that which is to come: and **hath put all things under His feet, and gave Him to be the head over all things to the church, which is His body, the fullness of Him that filleth all in all."** Let me put in layman's terms what this scripture says. The person, who believes the word of God, has the same power flowing toward him as Jesus had toward Him when

God raised Him from the dead and set Him at His own right hand in heavenly places. It also declares that because Jesus was raised up high above principality, and power, and might, and dominion, and every name that is named, and has had all things put under His feet, which is us, for we are His body, the fullness of Him that filleth all in all, **we are raised** far above these principalities, and powers, and might, and dominion, and every name that is named. In other words, because **Jesus has power and authority over these things,** including these beings, **so do we.** All we have to do is believe it and then take that authority over them when they get in our way. They may have the right to attack men, but **through Jesus Christ,** humans have a higher right, power, and authority to tell them to leave us alone. That is a privilege the body of Christ has because we are in Him and He earned that right when He spoiled principalities, and powers (Colossians 2:15).

If you believe that name will work and you use it, it will work. It is the most powerful name known in heaven and in earth. "It is the name from which the whole family is named, in heaven and in earth" (Ephesians 3:14-15).

I used to worry about invaders from outer space. I thought what if there are aliens. Then I realized the scripture said that the beings above the earth are subject to the name of Jesus. Aliens from outer space, if they are real, are still subject to the name of Jesus. God is not just the God of earth; He is the God of everything. He is the creator of everything. If there are beings from other planets, while on the earth, they are still subject to the name of Jesus. Therefore, they are nothing to be afraid of for the believer, because that is our name and they have to do what we say in that name.

# CHAPTER 8

# The war

2 Corinthians 10:3-5, "For though we walk in the flesh, we do not war after the flesh: (for the weapons of our warfare are not carnal, but mighty through God to the pulling down of strongholds,) casting down imaginations, and every high thing that exalts itself against the knowledge of God, and bringing into captivity every thought to the obedience of Christ."

We are at war while we are in the flesh. However, we are not talking about war with people, but rather these spirits. Remember their job is to afflict, oppress, destroy, attack, do battle, cause to sin, and cause trouble with men. If you are afflicted, oppressed, facing destruction, coming under some kind of attack, fighting sin, or trouble seems to follow you around, it maybe you are in war with one or more of these spirits. The word of God tells us how to win the war and stop the attacks.

# The Armor

Luke 11:21-23, "When a strong man **armed** keepeth his palace, his goods are in peace; but when a stronger than him shall come upon him, and overcometh him, he taketh from him all his armor wherein he trusted..." The armor spoken of is knowledge. Any person who is armed with knowledge (the purpose of this book is to arm the reader with knowledge) and stands against these unclean spirits can defeat them, keep them out, and get them out of their lives. James 4:7, "Resist the devil and he will flee from you." If the person knows what is going on and knows what to do, there will be a battle between the unclean spirit and the person. If the person stays in faith, and keeps his/her armor on, he/she will win. If the person is ignorant of these things (or is a dry place void of the word of God), the man has no armor to fight with. The spirit comes in and possesses the man's body and ruins or spoils his life.

God is providing armor for us to wear in our conflict against these evil spirits. This armor is mentioned in Ephesians 6:10-17, "Finally my brethren, be strong in the Lord and in the power of His might. Put on the whole armor of God that you maybe able to stand against the wiles of the devil. For we wrestle not against flesh and blood, but against principalities, against powers, against rulers of the darkness of this world, against spiritual wickedness in high places. Wherefore take unto you the whole armor of God, that you maybe able to withstand in the evil day, and having done all, to stand. Stand therefore having your loins girt with the truth." You need to know what the truth is in order to be able to stand against these unclean spirits.

Ephesians 6:14, " ...And having on the breastplate of righteousness." This means to be doing what is right in the eyes of God. If you are deliberately walking in sin, you are in the devils territory and you are fair game.

Ephesians 6: 15, "...and your feet shod with the preparation of the gospel of peace." This means to walk in love according to God's word. The Bible says in 2 Timothy 2: 25-26, "in meekness, instructing those who oppose themselves (are in strife); if God peradventure will give them repentance to the acknowledgment of the truth; and that they may recover themselves out of the snare of the devil, who are taken captive by him at his will." This is simply saying if you are in strife with anyone, you are in Satan's snare and you can be taken captive at his will. He can come in any time he wants to if you are in strife and have not forgiven someone.

Ephesians 6:16, "Above all, taking the shield of faith, where with you shall be able to quench all the fiery darts of the wicked." This means you say no to anything the devil throws at you that is contrary to what God's word says.

Ephesians 6:17, "Take the helmet of salvation." This means to think salvation, meditate on salvation, study salvation, talk salvation, and let it rule your thought life. This word salvation doesn't mean just spiritually, but in every aspect of your life. It means deliverance from these unclean spirits and demons.

The last part of verse 17 says, "Take the sword of the spirit, which is the word of God." This sword is an offensive weapon. It is the only offensive weapon we are afforded, but with it we can move mountains, cross-raging rivers, and do exploits. 2 Corinthians 4 says, "The weapons of our warfare are not carnal, but mighty through God to the pulling down of strongholds." You cannot use physical weapons as guns, knives, syringes (used in fighting diseases), or the like in this warfare. You can't get a shot that will affect an unclean spirit. Even death does not affect them. They just leave that body and go looking for someone else to attack. No, the offensive weapon of our warfare is our words, if they are God's word, but these words are mighty through God to the pulling down of any strongholds these spirits have set up in our lives. Read the story of the temptation of Jesus in the wilderness and see if you can locate all the armor of God on Jesus.

**Choose the words you speak carefully**. They can make the difference as to whether you live or die. Proverbs 18:21, "Death and life are in the power of the tongue and those who love it will eat the fruit thereof." Our weapon against death is to speak life. When it looks like you are going to die, cast those thoughts down and speak words of life. David said in Psalms 118:17, "I shall not die, but live, and declare the works of the Lord." I have had to say that twice in the face of death, once when the doctors said there was a hundred percent chance of death. Use the word of God against these spirits, against evil thoughts, and bad situations.

The knowledge you need to be ready for any attack of these spirits is given in the last few versus of Ephesians 6:10-17: (1). Know the truth (once again the purpose of this book is to bring you the truth), (2). Walk in righteousness (known sin in a person's life is an open door to demon oppression and possession), (3). Walk in love (which is the gospel of peace), (4). Stand in faith (believe when you give the unclean spirit a command, it has to obey you (Mark 11:23-24), (5). Use the sword of the spirit (using scripture as Jesus did) against the spirit. The person who does this is armed, and depending on how strong they are in it, can keep the evil spirit out.

## Binding

Matthew 12:29, "If you are going to spoil a strong man's house you must first bind him." When ever I start a deliverance on someone, I speak to the spirit and say you are bound in Jesus' name from getting violent and jumping on me or attacking me in any way. When I do this, the person who has the unclean spirit acts like they have ropes or chains tying them down. In the ministry of deliverance, it is pretty common to be jumped on when the spirit manifest itself in the person receiving the deliverance. I stop that from happening to me by applying the law in Matthew 18:18, which says, "Whatever you bind on earth, will be bound in heaven."

In one of the deliverances I was performing, you could see the spirit (using the person's body) striving against unseen bonds as though they were going to break them and come attack me. So I got a saint who was with me to say to the spirit, "I agree with Brother Ramsey, you are bound and cannot move in Jesus' name." The person (needing the deliverance) locked up like someone had thrown chains around her and fell over on the couch. She couldn't even wiggle until we got the spirit out of her. She had a spirit named Destruction in her. That was why Jesus sent the apostles and disciples out by twos. He knew that no evil spirit could with stand them if the two would agree together in faith.

You see the words are to the spirit controlling the person and not the person. You can stop anything these spirits are doing to you by binding them. Simply say, "Stop doing that (whatever it is they are doing), now in Jesus' name." If the person doing this thing to you is under the control of one of these unclean spirits, they will also stop because you have forbid the spirit from doing that to you. I have heard of women who were about to be raped scream out, "You get off of me in the name of Jesus and leave me alone." The man would immediately get off of them and run away as though the police were after them.

Matthew 18:18, "Verily I say unto you, that whatsoever you bind on earth will be bound in heaven: and whatsoever you loose on earth will be loosed in heaven." This scripture gives us the power to allow things to happen and the power to stop things from happening on earth. The word "bind" comes from the Greek word "deo." It means to bind, fasten with chains, throw into chains, to forbid, prohibit, declare to be illicit. This scripture is then saying to us whatever we (as men/women) bind, prohibit, or forbid these spirits to do, they cannot do and it is backed up by heaven itself. They can be stopped from oppressing, afflicting, destroying, attacking, and doing battle with us by the words of our mouth binding them. Simply say to the spirit, "I bind you in Jesus' name from oppressing, afflicting, destroying, attacking, and doing battle with me."

You may not know if it is one of these spirits or not, say it any way. I remember seeing a mighty man of God one time working on a car engine, his son had a wreck on his bicycle and skinned his knee. After tending to him, the man turned around bumping his shin on the trailer hitch of the car he was working on. He stopped, closed his eyes, and said, "I rebuke you, you spirit causing these accidents in Jesus' name. You will not operate around this house or to this family any more." I don't know if there was a spirit involved in that or not, but there weren't any more accidents that day. That incident really impressed me. If you are tormented by bad dreams, visitations at night, apparitions, or such like, just speak to them and tell them to go away and never to come back again in Jesus' name. Just see God's word work on your behalf. Stop them from tormenting you.

# Breaking curses

Here is an important fact to everyone who has had a curse put on him or her. These assignments (curses) can be broken by taking authority (in Jesus' name) over the demon spirit carrying out the assignment and commanding them to stop whatever they are doing. Be very specific in what you are saying to the demon for they only have to obey what you tell them. You might want to include in your command to never come back to you again. They must obey the person standing by faith in God and in Jesus' name rather than the person using witchcraft because the law of faith is a higher law then the law of witchcraft. Witchcraft is a work of the flesh (Galatians 5:19), while faith comes from the spirit. The flesh is temporary; the spirit is eternal.

The second part of Matthew 18:18, "Whatsoever you loose on earth will be loosed in heaven" gives you the power to release these spirits. The word "loose" is the Greek word "Luo." It means to release anything tied or fastened, to loosen, undo, or dissolve, to annul or to subvert, to do away with, and to deprive of authority whether by precept or act. Sometimes you may need to loose the spirit. For instance, if a curse has been placed on you, your house, or something you own, you can loose it where it is no longer under authority to curse you or attack you. You deprive it of the authority to carry out its assignment. You annul its assignment. Curses are when someone assigns a demon against us to afflict us or even kill us in some way. When we loose that curse, we break it where it can no longer function against us. The spirit must leave us alone. If it is a loved one you believe has had a curse put on them, simple loose the spirit bringing on the curse. Annul its assignment, stop its purpose, and break its authority in Jesus' name. Say, "I speak to the demon spirit that is carrying out this curse. I break your assignment and command you in Jesus' name to leave my loved one (or me if it is you) alone, now and forever." The spirit will have to leave your loved one (or you) alone. If you bind a spirit and nothing happens, try loosing it. You might want to loose the spirit, if it's a curse, and then bind it from attacking you because it desires to.

## Testing Spirits

If you have a spirit appear to you as an angel, someone you know, or even Jesus, do not accept the spirit as being from God until you test it. The test (1 John 4:3) is the spirit *must confess <u>out loud</u> that Jesus Christ is come in the flesh.* I do not care how much like Jesus it looks or feels. Jesus will not be angry if you test Him because He has told us too in His word. He will be glad you knew the word and acted on it. You see, I have counseled with people who have had spirits appear to them they thought was Jesus until they gave it the test, and it wouldn't say Jesus Christ is come in the flesh. If the spirit hesitates, or delays, I would not accept it as being Jesus. If there is anyone who will act on His word, it is Jesus, and His word says to try the spirits.

If the spirit will not confess to you out loud that Jesus Christ is come in the flesh, don't believe it. Tell it to leave in Jesus' name and never come back! The Bible says that Satan himself can transform into an "angel of light" in 2 Corinthians 11:14. He is not an angel of light, but he can transform into one in order to deceive people.

## Spiritual Strength

When casting out unclean spirits, the results will depend on how strong the unclean spirit is in comparison to the spiritual strength (faith) of the person doing the ministering. Just like different people have different physical strengths, people will also have differing spiritual strengths and just like a person can increase their physical strength a person can increase their spiritual strength. Scripture proving this is Luke 1:80, when talking about John the Baptist says, "The child waxed strong in the spirit." Luke 2:40, talking about Jesus, Says He also, "waxed strong in the spirit." The amount of spiritual strength of the person ministering deliverances will determine how long it takes to get the spirit to leave the person or thing. If you are not strong enough, you will have to wear the unclean spirit down which weakens it. Just like in a fight, the spirit wears down, as it has to continually exert spiritual strength fighting against the one who is casting it out. If the one ministering the deliverance will stay with it and not doubt, the unclean spirit will have to come out. If the person ministering the deliverance is strong in God and strong spiritually, it won't take long in most cases to get them out. Usually, Jesus got them out almost instantly. Sometimes like in the case above about the mad man of Gadara, it took a while even for Jesus to get them out. I have had deliverances that lasted for hours and I have heard of some lasting for days. The stronger I become the less time it takes to get them to obey.

A spiritually strong person can keep a weaker unclean spirit out. A stronger unclean spirit can take over a weaker human's life. If you are weak spiritually, get help from someone who is spiritually strong. The characteristics of someone who is spiritually strong is found in 1 John 2:14, "I have written, unto you young men, for you are strong, and the word of God abideth in you, and you have overcome the wicked one." Some one strong is someone who has had time to grow up spiritually (not a novice or baby Christian), knows and has the word of God abiding in them, and have overcome the wicked one in their life. Paul told Timothy in 1Timothy 6:12 to, "Fight the good fight of faith." Ephesians 3:20, "Now unto Him who is able to do exceeding abundantly above all that we ask or think, **according to the power that worketh in us.**" Winning the battle against these spirits is not according to God's strength, but according to the power working in us. It is not all up to God. His power can do anything; we are the ones lacking in power. It is according to the power (strength) working in us.

One way I increase my spiritual strength is by praying in tongues. I do this when alone, but I have been known to do it while ministering deliverance to someone. I have found that there is nothing that gets a demon to manifest or get stirred up better than speaking in tongues. I have had more evil spirits, through the person jump on me while I was praying in tongues over them. I don't know why that riles the evil spirits up so much. The Bible says in I Corinthians 14:4, "He that speaketh in an unknown tongue edifieth himself." The word edifies means to charge up like a battery, to become strong. If I know I am going to have to perform deliverance on someone, I pray in tongues as much as I can before I start the deliverance. When I get there, I am spiritually charged and strong. Some of the greatest miracles I have seen in my ministry came after spending hours the day before praying in tongues. The Bible also says in I Corinthians 14:17, that "he that prays in the unknown tongue gives thanks well." Other people can't understand it, but God can. Psalms 8:2 which says, "Out of the mouth of babes and sucklings has Thou ordained strength because of Thine enemies, that Thou mightest still the enemy and the avenger." In Matthew 21:16, Jesus quoted this scripture but instead of saying "out of the mouth of babes and sucklings hast Thou ordained strength," He says "out of the mouth of babes and suck-lings hast Thou perfected praise." The word translated strength in Psalms 8:2 can be translated praise and was translated praise by the Lord Jesus. So Psalms 8:2 says that out of the mouth of babes and sucklings (ones who don't have much strength) God ordained praise to give them strength that He might still the enemy and the avenger. That is why Paul wrote in I Thessalonians 5:18, "In everything give thanks, for this is the will of God in Christ Jesus concerning you." He wasn't saying the trouble you were having was His will, He was saying the giving thanks in everything was His will. Why? So He might still the enemy and the avenger for you. Praying in tongues (in the spirit as Paul says) is a great way to increase your spiritual strength or edify yourself.

## A step further

It is important for you to understand you have to do more than just say I rebuke you. Many Christians have done this only to loose the battle. They ask, "Why?" Here is the reason why. When you say, "I rebuke you," you have not told the spirit or person or thing what to do or not to do. When Jesus rebukes the winds and the waves, He doesn't say, "I rebuke you," He says, "Peace be still." Saying, "Peace be still" is the rebuke. If your child is drawing on the living room wall and you come in and scream and say, "Johnny, I rebuke you." Will he stop? No, probably not. But when you say, "Johnny stop drawing on that wall" then you have rebuked him and he should stop. The devil is the same way only he **will** stop.

In the early years of my deliverance ministry, I was ministering deliverance to a good friend of mine. He wanted to believe in God, but couldn't. He came to Bible studies but just didn't believe in God. It was peculiar though, for he did believe there was a supreme being but it wasn't God. In one Bible study, I asked him if I could pray for him. He agreed. The Spirit of God was leading me to minister deliverance to him and that was where I was headed. I bowed my head and began praying for him in tongues. All of a sudden I heard him growl and looked up at him (don't ever close your eyes when praying for someone who needs deliverance: that is a good time to do what Jesus said when he said, "Watch and pray.") He was flying at me. He had jumped up out of the chair and was attacking me. His eyes were solid red and he looked like a wolf attacking, with such hate in his eyes. I said, "I rebuke you in Jesus' name" twice and nothing happened. I thought, "Oh my God, I have gotten a hold of one that is not subject to the name of Jesus." He had practically pulled my shirt over my head, but I managed to get loose from him by ripping my shirt away from him. I now stood in the middle of the floor between him and the front door. I thought, I will give it one more shot and if it doesn't work, I am running out the front door. I shouted, "You sit down right there." He instantly stopped where he was. Now being in control, I went ahead with the deliverance. I had the unclean spirit in manifestation so I asked him his name. He said, "My name is Argon." I asked him, "What do you minister?" He said, "The real truth." I asked, "What is the truth?" He said, "God is not God." Remember, this man wanted to believe in God but couldn't? If you are a loved one doesn't believe in God, this spirit of Argon is probably attached or in you or them. If you are witnessing to someone like this, take a moment to bind the spirit from ministering to him or her where they can't believe in God. This spirit wouldn't allow him to believe in

God. I cast the spirit out of him and the man immediately believed in God, accepted Jesus as his savior, and was filled with the Holy Ghost. This was before I knew to tell the spirits not to come back. The man walked with God for a short while, but the spirit began to tell him those things never happened because he didn't remember them. He confessed there was a time span missing from his memory on that night, but he didn't believe that what his wife, my wife, and I said happened really happened. He finally accepted Argon back in and from that time on never even wanted to believe in God.

I told you this true story to show you saying "I rebuke you" is not enough. You must tell them to stop, now, and forever. If you don't tell your child, "Never draw on the wall again," he might come back the next day and draw on the wall. The devil is the same way. He will have to stop what he is doing, but if you don't tell him not to come back, he has followed your instructions to the "t," but can come back later.

## Where to send them

When casting out spirits, be cautious as to where you send them. Some send them to the abyss, or Russia. Don't do that. First of all, it is unscriptural to send them to the abyss. Jesus didn't do it and neither should we. Be specific as to what they cannot do. I will not allow them to stay in my hometown as that is my place of habitation and it is on the earth. I will not allow them to enter into any of my family or the person's family I am ministering too. I also will not allow them to enter into any of their animals. I used to tell them to go to the dry places, but you don't have to, as that is where they go any way. If I think someone is particularly vulnerable to a spirits attack, I will not allow the unclean spirit to attack that person. They have to do what I command as long as it is on the earth. You have the same dominion and authority. If it is your house, tell them to leave your house now and never come back in Jesus' name. You have dominion and authority over your house and over your possessions.

# CHAPTER 9

# Casting out of demons

Every deliverance from unclean spirits is different. You never know what to expect. Even in the Bible, the accounts of Jesus casting out unclean spirits had different occurrences. You need to be ready for anything! If you are going to be ministering deliverance, I highly encourage you to read this book until you are fairly familiar with it. Read especially the instructions and actual deliverances I have told about. There is knowledge in these events. The things written in this book should have you ready for just about any manifestation that could occur. I want to go over the main protocol I usually follow when casting out unclean spirits. It has worked for me for many years without me getting hurt. I am not saying, my technique is the only way or even the best way to minister deliverance. It is just my way and it works.

Please understand this, this is not fun and games. I used to think it was cool to be able to cast out demons. That was because I really didn't understand about them or what they could do. I am fully persuaded that if God had not been with me in my ignorance, I would have been killed several times by the demon possessed person. Please do not take this lightly. This is no game. However, it is something that needs to be done, sometimes, in order to save someone's life from torment, anguish, insanity, and maybe even death.

My first suggestion is to not do this alone. Have at least one person with you whom you believe to be a strong believer. Try to get someone who has studied this book or has done deliverance before. Jesus sent the disciples out by twos to cast out devils. Have more than one if possible, but no more than two or three. Never minister to someone of the opposite sex by yourself unless you just have too. Try to have someone else of the same sex as the person you are ministering to with you. I say this because you never know what kind of trick these unclean spirits will pull on you and it is better to protect yourself. It might be that the person of the opposite sex's flesh might rise up or they might have a spirit of sexual perversion. They might do something that will catch you off guard and make you very vulnerable to their sexual attack. It is possible for the unclean spirits to use sexual means to distract you and get you off the intended track and try to get you into sexual sin.

I would be very careful about the people you allow in the room with the person you are ministering too. I have heard it said that if there are other people in the room with unclean spirits that they can draw strength from one another. I do not know this to be true, but it is possible. This is one more good reason to have a select group of people in the room with you when ministering deliverance.

Lets say I am going to minister deliverance to an individual whose name is Fred. The first thing I would do is speak to the spirit/ spirits inside Fred. I would say out loud something like; "I speak to the strong man/strong men in Fred, and I bind you in Jesus' name. You will **not** be violent and attack or harm anyone or anything in this house. You will **not** harm Fred in any way." You never know how many spirits you may have to deal with. In the mad man of Gadara (Mark 5:9; Luke 8:30), there was only one strong man. I assumed for years that if there were only one strong man in the mad man of Gadara, there would only be one strong man in everyone who was "possessed." This assumption may not be true. There is no scripture that says this is true.

When you tell the spirit/spirits it can't get violent etc. you are binding it and it can't do whatever it is you told it. I would also suggest, that you get a believer that is with you to agree with you by speaking to the spirit (when speaking to the spirit, it will be like speaking to the person who is possessed by the demon) out loud and saying, "I agree with brother So-and-so or sister So-and-so. You are bound in Jesus' name. You will not get violent or harm anyone or anything in this house." When you get rid of the strongman of the house, its whole household has to go out with it. I say this, because

Jesus was only talking to the strong man in the mad man of Gadara called Legion, but when it left, the whole legion of demons left with it. Jesus did not deal with every demon in the man; He only dealt with the strong man.

The next thing I do is command the strongman to manifest itself without getting violent or aggressive. I like to do this to know I am dealing with an unclean spirit or that there is one present. When I do this, they will usually cause some kind of reaction in the person's body. Jerks, thoughts, actually speaking out loud, feelings of anger, hate, (usually of me), or a sudden pain somewhere are some of the things they may experience. I take these as signs I am dealing with an unclean spirit. Sometimes I have to ask the person if they feel or think anything, but sometimes, God allows me to feel what they feel and I know what kind of sign the unclean spirit is exhibiting. If the spirit speaks to me, I always **ask its name and how many unclean spirits are present in the individual**. The reason I do this, is because Jesus did it to the mad man of Gadara. I don't know why He did it to him and not to all, but there might be a good reason. So I do it to all unclean spirits I get to manifest through the voice. Plus, when I have them "on the line" so to say, I can learn more about them and how they operate. I may not get them to give me a name or the number. I assume that if they don't give me their name and/or the number of spirits in the person, then they don't have too. However, they do have to obey me and come out of the person. It might be they are a type of unclean spirit that cannot talk. When they use the person's voice, anyone in the room can hear what they say. However, not all unclean spirits speak through the person.

I try to get almost every spirit to speak to me. Sometimes, they will speak to the person on the inside, but I can't hear it. They have to relay to me what they hear. I will ask them, "Did you hear anything?" You have to be led by the Holy Ghost on this. If you don't feel a leading to get the spirit to talk, then don't. As in all things, just follow the leading of the Holy Spirit.

Once I do all this, I command the unclean spirit to come out of them **now** and to stay out of them forever. I am very specific about what I tell them to do. I am in charge and they have to do what I tell them to do, but they only have to do exactly what I **tell** them to do. If I don't tell them, they don't have to do it. They are very legalistic and are only required to follow your commands. If you tell them to stand on their head in the corner right now, they will go to the corner and stand on their head. Therefore, make sure you cover all your bases when dealing with them.

You have to be very careful about not letting them go into the person's animals if they have any. I was ministering deliverance to a lady at her house one time. I had the spirit manifested and was struggling with it to get it out, when her little dog walked between her and I. Her gaze was immediately on the dog. I knew the spirit was planning to enter into the dog. Remember, the unclean spirits in the mad man of Gadara, wanted to enter into the pigs. I spoke to the spirit and said, "No, you will not enter into that dog." The spirit started wailing and crying like it had just lost its last hope. It had been wailing and saying, "But I don't want too" when I would tell it to leave her, before the dog walked by. The spirit and its household (she had more than one spirit in her) came out and the women felt so different on the inside. She came up to me the next Sunday and said she didn't know how to react any more. She said, "Things that should make me mad, don't make me mad any more." She said, "I don't even know how to feel any more." There was a real change in her life and she could instantly feel the difference.

You also have to be careful not to let them go into any of their family members who may not be strong enough to keep them out. I was ministering to a man one night and had an unclean spirit "on the line." He (the spirit) told me, "You don't know who you are messing with." I told it, "I don't care who you are, Jesus is greater than you and you have to bow your knee to His name, so you come out of him and go to the dry places in Jesus' name." The spirit spoke back and said, "The dry places are closer than you think." I knew it was talking about his teenage children. So I told it, "You will not enter into any of his family members or any one in this town. This is my town, and I will not allow you to live in this town ever again." That covered his entire family as well as mine as we all lived in that town.

When the spirits come out of a person, there may or may not be a strong manifestation. Sometimes, there will just be a quiet and a peace in the room and on the inside of the person. Sometimes, the person may dry heave or spit up the unclean spirits. Sometimes, the person may go into a type of convulsions and writhe upon the floor. Sometimes, the spirits may scream, wail, cry a loud, or just yell when coming out. The person may froth at the mouth, drool, or spit. Sometimes, they tear the person when coming out. The person will be sore the next day. However, some of these things may happen and it not be the spirit coming out. When we began looking at outward evidences that the spirit is coming out, we get into an area where we can be deceived. I have had this happen to people, but the spirit hadn't come out, but had caused the person to do this trying to deceive me into thinking they were gone so I would turn my faith off or quit applying pressure on them. Unclean spirits will also talk through the person telling you, "they (the unclean spirit) are gone and everything is ok." Of course they are lying. It is the spirit and not the person talking. To make sure you are dealing with the person, test the spirit using the method I spoke of in an earlier chapter. If they will not confess or are slow to confess that Jesus Christ is come in the flesh, it is not the person, but the evil spirit. Continue with the deliverance. The spirit may also speak and beg you to stop, making you think it is the person's wishes. Once again, try the spirit to see who it is that is talking. If they easily say, "Jesus Christ is come in the flesh" then it is the person talking and not the spirit. The spirit cannot say, "Jesus Christ is come in the flesh" (I John 4:1-3).

How do I know then the spirit is gone? I go by my inward feelings. You see, when I am casting out an unclean spirit, my spirit is battling with the unclean spirit so there is a battle going on inside me. I can feel when the spirit is leaving because it is like a tug of war. I feel them start slipping out. I don't know if everyone can feel that or not. I didn't notice it when I first started ministering deliverance, but after many experiences, I began to notice that feeling of the tug of war going on inside me. I keep my faith turned on and the pressure on until I feel the spirit leave. That feels kind of like it feels when your team starts pulling the other team in the mud in tug of war. Once they start sliding in, it goes pretty easily from there. The person you are ministering to will also feel a weight lifted off of them or a peace when the spirit is gone. They will definitely feel a difference. How much of a difference will be determined by how big an influence the unclean spirit had in their lives. Ministering deliverance is a lot like praying until you break through. The Pentecostals have a saying of "pray through." That means they keep praying until they break through the problem and know on the inside they got a hold of God. In them, the answer is sure and there is a great peace. You have to do deliverance the same way. Stick with it until you know on the inside the battle is won and the spirit is gone.

I don't minister deliverance to any one unless they desire it. I don't know if you can cast an unclean spirit out of someone who doesn't want it out. My thoughts are, "If they don't want the spirit to leave, but you go ahead and cast it out, they will let it back in." Jesus says they "will bring seven other spirits worse than them and the state of the person will be worse than before." This is a sticky situation though because sometimes it is the unclean spirits ministering to them the fact that they don't want deliverance. In ministering to a girl, one time, about giving her life back to Jesus, she said, "No, I am not ready to give up my marijuana and drinking." By the leading of God, I asked her if I could just pray for her. She said, "Yes," not knowing what I was going to do. I grabbed her hands and said out loud, "I bind the strong man in her that is telling her she doesn't want to give her life back to Jesus." I then said to her, "Are you ready to get right with God now?" She looked at me and tried to hear that voice telling her she didn't want to give up her drinking and marijuana. She heard nothing. I said, "You don't hear that voice saying you don't want to quit the sin in your life do you?" She said, "No! I don't." I asked, "Are you ready to get right with God and receive the gift of the Holy Ghost?" She said, "I sure am." I prayed, she got right with God, and the Holy Ghost entered her and she spoke in tongues. Sometimes, it is the unclean spirit that is keeping people from getting right. However, it is not always a spirit. Sometimes, it is just the person's flesh.

There was a lady in our town that was constantly coming to my co-pastor and myself for deliverance. She had numerous affairs and thought she had a spirit that was causing her to commit adultery. The co-pastor and myself prayed about it separately, and God told us both, "The problem was not a spirit, but her flesh." It was easier to blame her sin on an evil spirit rather then take the blame for her own fleshly lust. It would be easier to have a devil cast out of her than it would be to "crucify the flesh with the lust and affections thereof" as we are told to do in the Bible. Crucifying the flesh hurts and it hurts for a pretty long time sometimes. It is a real battle. Remember the word says in I Peter 4:1 "... he that hath suffered in the flesh, has ceased from sin." If there is no suffering in the flesh, there is no ceasing from sin.

One more thing I want you to understand. The person being ministered to is also in a battle. The spirit is trying to rip, tear, take over, hold onto, and many other things. The spirit is speaking to them all kinds of negative things. It can be very tiring for them. If they tell you during a lull in the battle, they are tired and want to quit, you need to quit until another time. However, as I have said before, test the spirit to make sure it is the person speaking and not the unclean spirit.

Sometimes when an unclean spirit manifests itself in a person, the person will have no memory or recollection of what he may have done. I ministered to a man who attacked me and when it was over, he never remembered jumping on me, pinning me to the floor, swinging at me, or talking to me. Sometimes the manifestations are that strong. It is possible that an unclean spirit can rise up in a person and cause them to do things they don't even know they are doing. They will do things they don't remember doing. I heard a story of a father who was bathing his child and all of a sudden realized he had drowned the child. He didn't know why or even remember doing it. They don't remember doing it if they are under the control of an evil spirit. I am fully persuaded that many psychopathic killers have a spirit of murder in them and that is how they can do the things they do. I am not saying all murderers have evil spirits in them, but some do. I always think when I hear someone say, "Something told me to do it" that they are probably telling the truth. That does not give them an excuse; however, they need to resist those thoughts or voices. If you are someone who hears these voices or does evil things you don't remember doing, you need to start speaking to the spirit causing this and telling them to come out of you in Jesus' name and never minister to you again. You need to do this before hurting someone else, ruining your life, or hurting yourself.

If you are abducted by someone who has this spirit and is planning to torture you or hurt you, take authority over it and command it not to hurt you in any way or touch you, and to let you go. Many have been in situations like this and use Jesus' name this way. Their abductors let them go and get away from them as fast as possible. If someone you know or love is abducted, say out loud the same thing.

I believe there to be a spirit of suicide that coerces some people to commit suicide. I am not saying evil spirits coerce all suicides, but I do believe they coerce some. If you have to fight thoughts and feelings of suicide, you might speak to the spirit of suicide in Jesus' name and tell it to leave you alone, and not to minister to you again. If it is a spirit of suicide, it will stop. You maybe surprised at the absence of the notion to kill yourself. If you are, then it was a spirit trying to get you to kill yourself. If you will remember, this is one of the jobs of the evil spirit.

Learn to follow the leading of the Lord. Most of my knowledge has come through God showing me what to do in actual deliverance situations. Remember I said no two deliverance episodes are the same. You need to have God to direct you in what you do.

I think it is important to address the issue of whether a Christian can be demon possessed or not. Many believe that a Christian cannot have an evil spirit because an evil spirit cannot dwell in the same place as the Spirit of God. I agree with this assessment, however, we need to clarify where the Spirit of God abides.

A Christian can have an evil spirit in their body and in their mind, but not in their spirit. The Spirit of God abides on the inside of the spirit of man. Some want to call a Christian who has an unclean spirit "oppressed" rather than "possessed." I don't know what you would call it, but I know that Christians can have evil spirits in them, that is, in their bodies. I have ministered deliverance to many Christians who have had unclean spirits. I have noticed, however, that the strength of the manifestation is worse for a nonbeliever than it is for a believer. I don't know if this is a rule or not, it is just something I have noticed in my ministry. However, I have not ministered deliverance to a lot of lost people.

To better understand where Jesus resides and where an evil spirit can dwell, I will compare the New Testament temple (our bodies) to the temple God inhabited in the Old Testament. The temple made of wood, brass, gold, and silver in the Old Testament was a type and shadow of the temple God inhabits in this dispensation, the Christian.

The Old Testament temple had three rooms, the outer court, the Holy place, and the Holy of Holies. These were all symbolic of the Christian God lives in today. We are a soul, we have a spirit, and we live in a body.

The Holy of Holies is synonymous with the spirit of man. God lived in the Holy of Holies in the Old Testament temple, just like He lives in the spirit of man in the New Testament temple. Only the high priest could enter the Holy of Holies in the Old Testament and that only one time a year. This area was the area behind the veil. It was sacred. Even the high priest had to perform certain rituals to cover him lest he die when entering into the presence of God. They even tied a rope to his ankle when he entered behind the veil, so that if he died, they could drag his body out. Jesus entered into our Holy of Holies behind the veil for us according to the book of Hebrews. That means when we believed in Jesus (the word) He entered into our hearts to take up residence there.

The outer court is synonymous with our bodies. The common people could enter the outer court and even bring in animals for sacrifice into the court. Just like any person or animal could enter the outer court, unclean spirits can enter our outer courts (Our bodies) if we let it. The word says in Romans 6: 16, "Know ye not, that to whom you yield yourselves as servants to obey, his servants ye are to whom you obey; whether of sin unto death, or of obedience unto righteousness?" If you yield your body to an unclean spirit through sin, their servant you will be. They can take over you. They can possess your body whether you are a Christian or not. These sins are called "works of the flesh" in Galatians 5:19. That does not mean that everyone who sins is demon possessed. Some sin because that is what they want to do and this sin comes from the heart.

The following are descriptions of deliverance sessions. Read them carefully and try to find all the important steps in ministering deliverance that were incorporated and those that are missing.

I was ministering one evening to a lady with several people there. They were all believers, but when I was getting the spirit in the lady to manifest, I had spirits in three other people to manifest also. They did not attack me, but they could have. I ended up casting devils out of all three before the night was over. This was before the Lord instructed me how to keep the demon-possessed person from jumping on me. When ministering to the last one, the evil spirit inside him caused him to jump on me. He was sitting on the couch and I was on a folding chair setting right in front of him praying in tongues. The next thing I knew, he growled and jumped on me. This was totally unexpected. I went over backwards and he landed on top of me with his knees pinning my arms to the floor. I was help-less for a moment. He was swinging at me for all he was worth, but his punches landed beside my head. He never hit me because God protected me. I wrestled my way out from under him and told him, "Lay down in the floor in Jesus' name." He obeyed. I had the spirit manifested so I commanded it to identify itself. It said, "I am Satan and I am more than you can handle." I said, "I didn't come in my name, I came in the name of Jesus and you can't handle Him or that name. Now you come out of him right now and never come to him again in Jesus' name." The spirit left. The man was now himself and he said, "How did I get down here?" "I was sitting on the couch the last thing I remember."

When pastoring the church in Andrews, I had a lady call me one day who had attended my church. She said her ex-husband's wife had just called her and said her husband had gotten his shotgun and was on his way to Andrews to shoot her. He lived in Big Spring, which was 63 miles away. She said the ex-husband was a very violent man and would do what he set out to do. I told her to call the police, but she said it wouldn't do any good because he would do what he had planned to do. She said he would find a way. She wanted me to pray. Under the leading of the Holy Ghost I prayed with her over the phone. I said, "I bind the evil spirit that is driving this man to come to Andrews and kill this woman." I said, "I command you in Jesus' name to cause him to turn around and go back home." I hung up and waited. I was a little anxious because I had never been in this situation before and I was concerned for the life of the women. I had to work hard to cast the care of it off on God. Several hours later, she called me and said that her ex-husbands wife called back and said he had come back home. She said that he had got half way to Andrews and suddenly turned around and went back to Big Spring. His wife asked him why and he said, "I don't know, I just had too." **He was**

**under the control of an evil spirit, and I had authority over the evil spirit, so he had to do what ever I told the evil spirit to do.** Notice, this authority worked over a distance also. I could not say directly to the man to turn around and go back home, but the spirit apparently heard me even from a distance. I remind you that Jesus cast the unclean spirit out of a woman's daughter from long distance by proxy through the woman (Matthew 15:28). I could speak to the unclean spirit through the man's ex-wife. I don't know if it would have worked or not if I hadn't had someone to act as a proxy. You have the same authority. Use it!

I received a phone call one night from a dear brother of my church. He sounded strange over the phone. I did not recognize that anything was wrong at first, but as I continued talking to him, I could tell there was something wrong. I asked him what was the matter and he responded with "I don't know." I asked him what was going on? He said, "I don't know." I asked, "Are you all right?" He answered, "I don't know." I knew then that I was talking to an evil spirit and not the man. I lived 10 miles from town and was in bed. I was afraid this spirit might do something to this man or cause him to hang up the phone before I could help him. I instantly said, "In the name of Jesus, do not put down this phone! You sit down where you are and wait until I can get there." I was a good 30 minutes from this man's house. I hung up the phone and got out of bed, got dressed, and drove to his house. I knocked on the front door and one of his children answered the door. I ask, "Where is your father?" The child said, "In his bedroom." I went into his bedroom and found him setting in the floor, in the corner, next to the phone, with the phone held up to his ear. He had been sitting there like that for nearly an hour. It really shocked me for I had never had anything like that happen to me. I told him to put the phone down and I began ministering deliverance to him. I am telling this story to show you how much authority and power you can have over these unclean spirits if you believe God's word.

## CHAPTER 10

# The greatest deliverance
# I ever witnessed

I have told you some of this story in bits and pieces, but I believe I am supposed to tell the whole story in its entirety. It was 1985 and I was going to Odessa College to finish my Associates degree. I had met a girl there who was a classmate of mine. I was witnessing to her about the Lord. She said she had accepted the Lord when she was younger and had back slidden since. We started talking about deliverance and evil spirits when she told me she felt like she needed deliverance. I don't remember why she felt that way, but I asked her if she wanted deliverance, if she needed it. She said, "Yes." I began to minister right there on the Odessa College campus. I commanded the spirit to manifest. This was before I knew to bind the spirit to keep it from getting violent with me. Any way, nothing happened. I ask her if she felt anything and she said that she felt kind of jittery in her stomach. I took this as being the manifestation I was looking for. I spoke to the strong man saying, "Strongman, identify yourself in Jesus' name." I heard nothing, but she said, "He is speaking to me." I said, "What is he saying?" She said, "He says his name is Argon." I had never heard of that name before, but knew it had to come out because she didn't want it and I was going to tell it to come out in Jesus' name. I did, he did, and she felt him leave. That was on Friday.

The following Monday, we were having a Bible study at one of my best friend's house. He, his wife, his sister and her husband, and my wife and I were there. We were talking before the study started when my friend made the statement that he really didn't believe in God. We all pounced on that like a bird on a June bug. He said that he wished he could believe like us and that was why he participated in these Bible studies. He said he just couldn't believe in God. I asked him how the things of this world could have possibly been made without there being a supreme being to create it. He said, "Oh, I believe in a supreme being, I just don't believe in God." God began to lead me to minister deliverance to him. I asked him, "If you saw an evil spirit cast out of a person, would you believe in God?" He said, "I don't think I would actually have to see the evil spirit come out. If I could just see the evidences of it, I think I would have to believe." I said, "Wouldn't it be funny if it came out of you?"

I excused myself to go to the bathroom because I needed to talk to God in private. I knew what God was leading me to do but

I also knew that if nothing happened, he would be driven farther into unbelief. I prayed Father, "I know what you want me to do. However, if nothing happens he will be driven farther into unbelief." God spoke to me as I opened the bathroom door and said, "Start talking to him about deliverance." I said, "Ok Lord, but I ask You to give me a supernatural intercession for him so I could know what he is feeling." I knew I was heard of God and this was God's go ahead with the plan.

I did what God told me to do and came to a place where I asked him if I could pray for him. He said, "Yes." He was setting in his easy chair and I was setting in a kitchen chair pulled up close enough that I could hold both his hands while I prayed for him. This was in order to make contact so I could feel what he was feeling. I commanded the spirit in him to manifest. I asked him if he felt anything. He said, "No, not really." I said, "Yes, you did." He asked, "What?" I said, "You felt a jerk in your right forearm, right there." He said, "I can't deny that." I then bowed my head, closed my eyes, and started praying in tongues. This was a bad mistake. Never take your eyes off of the person you are ministering to when ministering deliverance to them. The next thing I heard was a scream coming from him and he was all over me. He was trying to get his hands around my throat. I managed to stand up. This had never happened to me before, and I thought I had made him mad by praying in tongues. Just as soon as that thought entered my mind, the Spirit of God spoke to me and told me it was that spirit attacking me. I didn't know they would do that. When he jumped on me, his wife grabbed their baby and went one way and my wife grabbed my baby and ran the other way. I was all alone fighting for my life. He was frothing at the mouth, growling and clawing at me like a wild animal. He had a hold of my shirt and just about had it over my head.

I said, "I rebuke you in Jesus' name," and nothing happened. I said it again. Nothing happened. He was still coming after me. I thought, "Oh my God, I have gotten a hold of an evil spirit the name of Jesus' has no power over." He only had my shirt so I knew that was my chance to get away from him. I pulled loose and managed to get some space between him and me. I was terrified. My knees were shaking so bad I could hardly stand up. My voice was shaking so bad I could hardly make myself speak. I thought, "I am going to give this one more shot and if it doesn't work, I am going out the front door because this thing will kill me." I mustered up the strength to say with a shaky voice, "You sit down right there in Jesus' name." Up until then, he was approaching me cautiously and was crouched like a wolf walking on his hind legs. His eyes had turned red and he had such hate flowing out at me.

He stopped. He didn't sit down there, but he stopped. I knew then that the name of Jesus did work on him. I began to gain my composure, but it made me mad. At this point, God spoke to me to have him lay down under the coffee table. I thought that was a dumb thought and so it had to be me and not God. I found out later how much God it really was.

I commanded him to go back to the chair he was sitting in and sit down. He obeyed. I got the same chair and scooted right up in front of him to let the spirit know I was not afraid of him. I said, "In the name of Jesus identify yourself." He said, "You know." I commanded it again, "Identify yourself in Jesus' name." He said, "You know, we've met before." I had cast out a few spirits before then but I didn't know which one this one was. He apparently was avoiding telling me his name so I thought this must be one that you have to have his name in order to command him to leave. I said, "I am going to ask you one more time who you are and you are going to have to tell me. I am going to wait right here until you do. Now, who are you?" He said, "Argon." I thought Argon! I didn't understand it and I still don't, but that was the same spirit I had cast out of the girl in Odessa College. Any way, I thought, I have got him "on the line" so I am going to find out something about him. I asked Argon, "What do you minister?" He answered, "The real truth." I asked, "Argon, what is the real truth?" He said, "God is not God." I said Argon, "You are a liar and the truth is not in you. Now you and your household have to leave him right now in Jesus' name." Then I sat back.

The man's face and eyes changed. I called his name and asked him if he knew what happened? He answered, "No, but I know something just happened." He had scrapped his knuckles in his fight with me and noticed it and asked how that happened. His wife, my wife, and I each told him what had happened from each standpoint. He said, "The last thing I remember was I hated you more than anything in this world and if I had a gun in this house, you would be dead now." He looked at the table beside the chair he was sitting in and his eyes got big. There was a Bible setting there beside the lamp and a pair of scissors beside the Bible. He said, "Man I don't know what happened. I remember looking on that table for something to kill you with. I saw the Bible and the lamp but I never saw the scissors." God protected me because I was foolish and had my head bowed and my eyes closed. If he had seen those scissors, he would have easily stabbed me with them. I learned to watch and pray whenever ministering deliverance.

I asked him what he was feeling now. He said, "I just know there are a lot of bad things outside that door and they want to get to me." I said, "Those are evil spirits that want back in. You need Jesus. Are you ready to pray and accept Him into your life?" He said, "Yes I am." I led him in the sinner's prayer. I then asked him if he would like to receive the gift of the Holy Ghost. He said that he wanted everything God had for him. I laid my hands on him and led him in a prayer asking for the Holy Ghost to come in. The Holy Ghost did, which was evidenced by the fact that he spoke in tongues. He was on fire for God for a few weeks. Than all of a sudden, he announced his unbelief of what happened that night. I tried to reason with him, but he wouldn't listen. I told him the Bible says, "When the unclean spirit comes back in, he brings seven other spirits worse than him, and the state of the man was worse than at the first." I asked, "You used to want to believe in God didn't you? But, now you don't, right?" He said, "That is true. I don't care now."

The spirit Argon had come back to him and convinced him that we were lying about what happened because we didn't see things the same way. He said that he knew something happened but he didn't believe it was what we said. If I had listened to God and had him lay down under the coffee table, there would be no way he could deny that we were telling the truth. Instead, I had him go back to the same chair he jumped out of. I pray that someday, this man will find deliverance again and find God back in his life.

I changed the way I did deliverance after that episode. God showed me in the word how I could command the spirit not to come back and they couldn't. I began doing that in all the deliverances I worked. It was not till a much later deliverance that the Lord showed me I could stop the spirit in the man from attacking me. Up until that time, I was jumped on many times. But it did not affect me like that time.

# CHAPTER 11

# Reigning in life as a king

Romans 5: 17, "…much more they, which receive abundance of grace and the gift of righteousness, shall reign in life by one, Christ Jesus." God wants you to reign in your life like a king. But, you are the one who has to take authority. You have to reign. Nowhere in the Bible does it say to pray to God and He will rebuke the devil. You are to resist these unclean spirits by the words of your mouth. You are to use your authority over these spirits. God the Father did not rebuke the devil for Jesus. Jesus had to do it for Himself. Jesus **said**, He didn't think, He didn't pray, He **spoke**, "It is written." God is not going to rebuke the devil for you. If you are a tither, Malachi 3:8-11 says God "will rebuke the devourer for your sake." It doesn't say He will rebuke the devil for you. You must rise up, take your stand, and tell the enemy as a king, "You will not torment or harass me any longer. Get out of my house and my life

now and stay out." Then stand firm in faith, telling him he has to go. No matter what happens, he has to go. If you feel or know you are too weak alone, get someone strong in the spirit to agree with you and to stand with you. The enemy has to obey. It is our blessing given to us as man. Bind them, tell them to stop, be authoritative. You can do it.

Before starting this book, I got a team of prayer warriors to pray for me in the writing of the book, and to agree with me that everyone who reads this book and applies it to their situation regarding any unclean spirit, demon, or ghost, that our faith would be joined with theirs to cause the unclean spirit or ghost to leave them alone. It is not just your strength involved; it is the strength of my prayer team and myself who will be fighting with you. Act on this book and see the power of God work in delivering you from these tormenting spirits and/or curses. God bless you and yours. Blessed is he who reads this book and acts on its principals, for it is of God.

Notes

Notes

Notes

Notes

Notes

# About the Author

The author was born in a small West Texas town by the name of Andrews. He was raised in a Christian home and was well acquainted with Jesus, the Bible, and prayer. He was taught to stand on the promises of God from an early age. He was saved at the age of 5 at a Southern Baptist Church and received the Gift of The Holy Ghost at the age of 19 at a Non-denominational Church in Andrews. His life changed completely at this time.

He began pastoring a church in 1974 where he preached for 19 years. In 1993, he went back to school and finished his education at The University of Texas of the Permian Basin. He received his Bachelor's degree in 1997 and graduated at the top of his class with a 3.95 GPA. He went on the get his Master's degree in 2003 in education.

During his tenure as a pastor, one of the ministries he was used in was the ministry of deliverance. He saw things a lot of people don't believe in as far as manifestations of evil spirits and demons.

He saw a lot of people set free from the torments of these spirits. He learned a lot about these spirits from experience and had the Lord to direct him in certain matters like the binding of the spirit to keep the person with the spirit from attacking him.

During this time, the reoccurring dreams where that he would be meeting someone face to face that he knew was Satan himself. In the dream, all he had to do was to keep quiet and Satan would have left him alone. However, he couldn't. He would say, "I know who you are and that your powers are evil." Then Satan would come after him to destroy him. He knew that all he had to do was say the name of Jesus, but he was so scared all he could say was "in the name of JeJeJeJeJe." He could never come out with the name. After a few years of studying the word and growing spiritually, he had a dream like that, but when he got to the saying the name of Jesus, he said it with authority and power. He has not had such a dream since. He says it was God getting him ready to face the devil one on one and to win using the name of Jesus. He feels, this book is an open confrontation with the forces of darkness and maybe paramount to him not being able to keep his mouth shut in his dream. However, if Satan and all the forces of darkness do retaliate, he stands on the scripture where Jesus said, "Behold, I give unto you power and authority to tread upon serpents and scorpions and over all the power of the enemy and nothing shall by any means hurt you." He also stands on the word "The angel of the Lord is encamped around those who fear Him, and delivers them,"

At the present he is a schoolteacher on the elementary level and ministers some at his brother's full-gospel church. He is an avid studier of God's word and has had revelations from God that has excited and awed the listeners who hear him.

To contact the author: E-Mail ramtam@sbcglobal.net